Zabriskie

THE YALE SHAKESPEARE

Revised Edition

General Editors

Helge Kökeritz and Charles T. Prouty

Published on the fund

given to the Yale University Press in 1917

by the members of the

Kingsley Trust Association

(Scroll and Key Society of Yale College)

to commemorate the seventy-fifth anniversary

of the founding of the society

THE YALE SHAKESPEARE

MEASURE FOR MEASURE

Edited by Davis Harding

NEW HAVEN : YALE UNIVERSITY PRESS

London: Oxford University Press

Library of Congress catalog card number: 54–5286

FIRST PUBLISHED, OCTOBER, 1926
REVISED EDITION, OCTOBER, 1954

Preface of the General Editors

AS the late Professor Tucker Brooke has observed, practically all modern editions of Shakespeare are 18th-century versions of the plays, based on the additions, alterations, and emendations of editors of that period. It has been our purpose, as it was Professor Brooke's, to give the modern reader Shakespeare's plays in the approximate form of their original appearance.

About half the plays appeared in quarto form before the publication of the First Folio in 1623. Thus for a large number of plays the only available text is that of the Folio. In the case of quarto plays our policy has been to use that text as the basis of the edition, unless it is clear that the text has been contaminated.

Interesting for us today is the fact that there are no act or scene divisions in the Quartos with the exception of *Othello*, which does mark Acts I, II, IV, and V but lacks indications of scenes. Even in the Folio, although act divisions are generally noted, only a part of the scenes are divided. In no case, either in Quarto or Folio, is there any indication of the place of action. The manifold scene divisions for the battle in such a play as *Antony and Cleopatra*, together with such locations as "Another part of the field," are the additions of the 18th century.

We have eliminated all indications of the place and time of action, because there is no authority for them in the originals and because Shakespeare gives such information, when it is requisite for understanding the play, through the dialogue of the actors. We have been sparing in our use of added scene and, in some

v

cases, act divisions, because these frequently impede the flow of the action, which in Shakespeare's time was curiously like that of modern films.

Spelling has been modernized except when the original clearly indicates a pronunciation unlike our own, e.g. *desart* (desert), *divel* (devil), *banket* (banquet), and often in such Elizabethan syncopations as *ere* (e'er), *stolne* (stol'n), and *tane* (ta'en). In reproducing such forms we have followed the inconsistent usage of the original.

We have also preserved much more of the original capitalization than is usual, for often this is a part of the meaning. In like manner we have tended to adopt the lineation of the original in many cases where modern editors print prose as verse or verse as prose. We have, moreover, followed the original punctuation wherever it was practicable.

In verse we print a final *-ed* to indicate its full syllabic value, otherwise *'d*. In prose we have followed the inconsistencies of the original in this respect.

Our general practice has been to include in footnotes all information a reader needs for immediate understanding of the given page. In somewhat empiric fashion we repeat glosses as we think the reader needs to be reminded of the meaning. Further information is given in notes (indicated by the letter *N* in the footnotes) to be found at the back of each volume. Appendices deal with the text and sources of the play.

Square brackets indicate material not found in the original text. Long emendations or lines taken from another authoritative text of a play are indicated in the footnotes for the information of the reader. We have silently corrected obvious typographical errors.

CONTENTS

[THE ACTORS' NAMES]

The scene: *Vienna*

The Names of All the Actors

VINCENTIO, *the Duke*
ANGELO, *the deputy*
ESCALUS, *an ancient lord*
CLAUDIO, *a young gentleman*
LUCIO, *a fantastic*
Two other like Gentlemen
[VARRIUS, *a gentleman attending on the Duke*]
Provost
THOMAS ⎫
PETER ⎭ *two friars*
[*A Justice*]
ELBOW, *a simple constable*
FROTH, *a foolish gentleman*
Clown [POMPEY, *tapster to Mistress Overdone*]
ABHORSON, *an executioner*
BARNARDINE, *a dissolute prisoner*

ISABELLA, *sister to Claudio*
MARIANA, *betrothed to Angelo*
JULIET, *beloved of Claudio*
FRANCISCA, *a nun*
MISTRESS OVERDONE, *a bawd*

[*Lords, Officers, Citizens, Boy, and Attendants*]

[The Actors' names] N.

MEASURE FOR MEASURE

Act I

SCENE 1

Enter Duke, Escalus, Lords [and Attendants].

Duke. Escalus.

Escalus. My lord.

Duke. Of government the properties to unfold,
Would seem in me t' affect speech and discourse,
Since I am put to know that your own science   5
Exceeds, in that, the lists of all advice
My strength can give you. Then no more remains,
But that, to your sufficiency, as your worth is able,
And let them work. The nature of our people,
Our city's institutions, and the terms   10
For common justice, y' are as pregnant in
As art and practice hath enriched any
That we remember. There is our commission,
From which we would not have you warp. Call hither,
I say, bid come before us Angelo.   15
                    [*Exit an Attendant.*]
What figure of us think you he will bear?
For you must know, we have with special soul
Elected him our absence to supply,

Act I N. (N refers throughout to the corresponding note given at the end of the text.) 3 **to unfold** read 't'unfold.' 4 **t' affect** to love. 5 **put** made. 6 **lists** limits. 8-9 **But . . . work** N. 11 **pregnant** expert. 14 **warp** deviate. 16 **figure** representation. 17 **soul** affection.

1

Lent him our terror, dress'd him with our love,
And given his deputation all the organs   20
Of our own power. What think you of it?
  Escalus. If any in Vienna be of worth
To undergo such ample grace and honor,
It is Lord Angelo.

Enter Angelo.

  Duke.   Look where he comes.
  Angelo. Always obedient to your Grace's will,   25
I come to know your pleasure.
  Duke.   Angelo,
There is a kind of character in thy life,
That to th' observer doth thy history
Fully unfold. Thyself and thy belongings
Are not thine own so proper, as to waste   30
Thyself upon thy virtues, they on thee.
Heaven doth with us as we with torches do,
Not light them for themselves; for if our virtues
Did not go forth of us, 'twere all alike   34
As if we had them not. Spirits are not finely touch'd
But to fine issues, nor Nature never lends
The smallest scruple of her excellence,
But, like a thrifty goddess, she determines
Herself the glory of a creditor,
Both thanks and use. But I do bend my speech   40
To one that can my part in him advertise.

19 **terror** i.e. authority to punish. 20 **deputation** vice-regency. 27 **character** hidden meaning (literally, cipher for secret correspondence). 29 **belongings** qualities. 30 **proper** exclusively. 30–1 **as to . . . thee** N. 32–3 **Heaven . . . themselves** N. 35 **Spirits** one syllable here, either 'spir'ts' or 'sprites.' **finely touch'd** nobly endowed. 36 **issues** purposes. 36–40 **Nature . . . use** N. 37 **scruple** third part of a dram. 38 **determines** decrees for. 40 **use** interest. 41 **one . . . advertise** (stressed — ⌣ —) N.

Hold therefore, Angelo:
In our remove be thou at full ourself.
Mortality and mercy in Vienna
Live in thy tongue and heart. Old Escalus,   45
Though first in question, is thy secondary.
Take thy commission.

   Angelo.   Now, good my lord,
Let there be some more test made of my mettle,
Before so noble and so great a figure
Be stamp'd upon it.

   Duke.   No more evasion.   50
We have with a leaven'd and prepared choice
Proceeded to you; therefore take your honors.
Our haste from hence is of so quick condition
That it prefers itself, and leaves unquestion'd
Matters of needful value. We shall write to you,   55
As time and our concernings shall importune,
How it goes with us, and do look to know
What doth befall you here. So fare you well:
To th' hopeful execution do I leave you
Of your commissions.

   Angelo.   Yet give leave, my lord,   60
That we may bring you something on the way.

   Duke. My haste may not admit it;
Nor need you, on mine honor, have to do
With any scruple. Your scope is as mine own,
So to enforce or qualify the laws   65
As to your soul seems good. Give me your hand.
I'll privily away. I love the people,

42 **Hold** N. 43 **remove** absence. 44 **mortality** death. 46 **question** appointment. **secondary** subordinate. 48 **mettle** essential worth; a quibble on 'metal.' 51 **We have** read 'We've.' **leaven'd** well-considered. 53–5 **Our . . . value** N. 56 **concernings** business. 61 **bring you something** escort you a short distance. 64 **scope** liberty to act.

3

But do not like to stage me to their eyes.
Though it do well, I do not relish well
Their loud applause and Aves vehement,   70
Nor do I think the man of safe discretion
That does affect it. Once more, fare you well.

Angelo. The heavens give safety to your purposes!

Escalus. Lead forth and bring you back in happiness!   74

Duke. I thank you. Fare you well.   *Exit.*

Escalus. I shall desire you, sir, to give me leave
To have free speech with you; and it concerns me
To look into the bottom of my place.
A power I have, but of what strength and nature
I am not yet instructed.   80

Angelo. 'Tis so with me. Let us withdraw together,
And we may soon our satisfaction have
Touching that point.

Escalus.   I'll wait upon your Honor.

                                             Exeunt.

SCENE 2

Enter Lucio and two other Gentlemen.

Lucio. If the Duke, with the other dukes, come not
to composition with the king of Hungary, why then
all the dukes fall upon the king.

1. Gentleman. Heaven grant us its peace, but not
the king of Hungary's!   5

68 **stage me** exhibit myself. 69 **do well** be fit. 70 **Aves** acclamations. 78 **bottom of my place** full extent of my authority. 2 **composition** agreement.

4

2. Gentleman. Amen.

Lucio. Thou conclud'st like the sanctimonious pirate, that went to sea with the Ten Commandments, but scraped one out of the table.

2. Gentleman. 'Thou shalt not steal'?   10

Lucio. Ay, that he razed.

1. Gentleman. Why, 'twas a commandment to command the captain and all the rest from their functions: they put forth to steal. There's not a soldier of us all that, in the thanksgiving before meat, do relish the petition well that prays for peace.   16

2. Gentleman. I never heard any soldier dislike it.

Lucio. I believe thee, for I think thou never wast where grace was said.

2. Gentleman. No? A dozen times at least.   20

1. Gentleman. What? In meter?

Lucio. In any proportion or in any language.

1. Gentleman. I think, or in any religion.

Lucio. Ay, why not? Grace is grace, despite of all controversy: as, for example, thou thyself art a wicked villain, despite of all grace.   26

2. Gentleman. Well, there went but a pair of shears between us.

Lucio. I grant: as there may between the lists and the velvet. Thou art the list.   30

1. Gentleman. And thou the velvet. Thou art good velvet; thou'rt a three-pil'd piece, I warrant thee. I had as lief be a list of an English kersey as be pil'd, as thou art pil'd, for a French velvet. Do I speak feelingly now?   35

16 petition . . . peace N. 22 proportion N. 27–8 there . . . us we were cut from the same cloth. 29 lists the outer edging made of plain material, pileless. 32 three-pil'd N. 33 kersey stout coarse cloth. 34 velvet courtesan. 35 feelingly to the purpose.

Lucio. I think thou dost; and indeed with most painful feeling of thy speech. I will, out of thine own confession, learn to begin thy health; but, whilst I live, forget to drink after thee.   39

1. Gentleman. I think I have done myself wrong, have I not?

2. Gentleman. Yes, that thou hast, whether thou art tainted or free.

Enter Bawd [Mistress Overdone].

Lucio. Behold, behold, where Madam Mitigation comes!   45

1. Gentleman. I have purchas'd as many diseases under her roof as come to—

2. Gentleman. To what, I pray?

Lucio. Judge.   49

2. Gentleman. To three thousand dolors a year.

1. Gentleman. Ay, and more.

Lucio. A French crown more.

1. Gentleman. Thou art always figuring diseases in me; but thou art full of error. I am sound.   54

Lucio. Nay, not—as one would say—healthy, but so sound as things that are hollow. Thy bones are hollow; impiety has made a feast of thee.

1. Gentleman. [*To Mistress Overdone.*] How now! Which of your hips has the most profound sciatica?

Mistress Overdone. Well, well; there's one yonder arrested and carried to prison was worth five thousand of you all.

2. Gentleman. Who's that, I pray thee?

36–9 and . . . thee N. 40 done myself wrong given myself away. 46–7 I . . . to N. 50 dolors pun on 'dollars.' 52 French crown a gold coin, a bald head. 59 sciatica regarded as a symptom of venereal disease.

6

Mistress Overdone. Marry, sir, that's Claudio, Signior Claudio.   65

1. Gentleman. Claudio to prison? 'Tis not so.

Mistress Overdone. Nay, but I know 'tis so. I saw him arrested, saw him carried away, and, which is more, within these three days his head to be chopp'd off.   70

Lucio. But, after all this fooling, I would not have it so. Art thou sure of this?

Mistress Overdone. I am too sure of it; and it is for getting Madam Julietta with child.   74

Lucio. Believe me, this may be. He promis'd to meet me two hours since, and he was ever precise in promise-keeping.

2. Gentleman. Besides, you know, it draws something near to the speech we had to such a purpose.

1. Gentleman. But most of all agreeing with the proclamation.   81

Lucio. Away! Let's go learn the truth of it.

          Exit [*Lucio with the Gentlemen*].

Mistress Overdone. Thus, what with the war, what with the sweat, what with the gallows and what with poverty, I am custom-shrunk.   85

Enter Clown [Pompey].

How now? What's the news with you?

Pompey. Yonder man is carried to prison.

Mistress Overdone. Well, what has he done?

Pompey. A woman.

Mistress Overdone. But what's his offense?   90

Pompey. Groping for trouts in a peculiar river.

84 sweat the plague. 85 custom-shrunk reduced to fewer customers. 89 woman N. 91 Groping . . . river N.

Mistress Overdone. What? Is there a maid with child by him?

Pompey. No, but there's a woman with maid by him. You have not heard of the proclamation, have you?   96

Mistress Overdone. What proclamation, man?

Pompey. All houses in the suburbs of Vienna must be pluck'd down.   99

Mistress Overdone. And what shall become of those in the city?

Pompey. They shall stand for seed: they had gone down too, but that a wise burgher put in for them.

Mistress Overdone. But shall all our houses of resort in the suburbs be pull'd down?   105

Pompey. To the ground, mistress.

Mistress Overdone. Why, here's a change indeed in the commonwealth! What shall become of me?

Pompey. Come, fear not you! Good counselors lack no clients. Though you change your place, you need not change your trade. I'll be your tapster still. Courage! There will be pity taken on you; you that have worn your eyes almost out in the service, you will be considered.   114

Mistress Overdone. What's to do here, Thomas Tapster? Let's withdraw.

Pompey. Here comes Signior Claudio, led by the provost to prison; and there's Madam Juliet.

                                                                        Exeunt.

*Enter Provost, Claudio, Juliet, Officers, Lucio,
and two Gentlemen.*

94 maid N. 98 suburbs N. 102 had gone would have gone. 103 put in interceded. 115–6 Thomas Tapster N. 118 provost jailor. SD Enter Provost . . . Gentlemen N. (SD is used throughout to indicate stage direction.)

Claudio. Fellow, why dost thou show me thus to th'
world?

Bear me to prison, where I am committed.   120

Provost. I do it not in evil disposition,
But from Lord Angelo by special charge.

Claudio. Thus can the demigod Authority
Make us pay down for our offense by weight
The words of heaven; on whom it will, it will;   125
On whom it will not, so: yet still 'tis just.

Lucio. Why how now Claudio? Whence comes this
restraint?

Claudio. From too much liberty, my Lucio, liberty.
As surfeit is the father of much fast,
So every scope by the immoderate use   130
Turns to restraint. Our natures do pursue,
Like rats that ravin down their proper bane,
A thirsty evil, and when we drink we die.

Lucio. If I could speak so wisely under an arrest,
I would send for certain of my creditors. And yet,
to say the truth, I had as lief have the foppery of
freedom as the mortality of imprisonment. What's
thy offense, Claudio?

Claudio. What but to speak of would offend again.

Lucio. What, is't murder?   140

Claudio. No.

Lucio. Lechery?

Claudio. Call it so.

Provost. Away, sir! You must go.

Claudio. One word, good friend. Lucio, a word with
you.   145

Lucio. A hundred, if they'll do you any good.

125 words of heaven N. 132 ravin swallow greedily. proper
bane poison peculiar to them. 136 foppery folly. 137 mortality
state of being subject to decay or death N.

9

Is lechery so look'd after?

Claudio. Thus stands it with me: upon a true contract

I got possession of Julietta's bed.

You know the lady; she is fast my wife,   150

Save that we do the denunciation lack

Of outward order. This we came not to,

Only for propagation of a dower

Remaining in the coffer of her friends,   154

From whom we thought it meet to hide our love

Till time had made them for us. But it chances

The stealth of our most mutual entertainment

With character too gross is writ on Juliet.

Lucio. With child, perhaps?

Claudio   Unhappily, even so.

And the new deputy now for the Duke—   160

Whether it be the fault and glimpse of newness,

Or whether that the body public be

A horse whereon the governor doth ride,

Who, newly in the seat, that it may know

He can command, lets it straight feel the spur;   165

Whether the tyranny be in his place,

Or in his eminence that fills it up,

I stagger in—but this new governor

Awakes me all the enrolled penalties   169

Which have, like unscour'd armor, hung by th' wall

So long that nineteen zodiacs have gone round,

And none of them been worn; and for a name

148 **contract** stressed — $\stackrel{\smile}{}$. 150 **she . . . wife** N. 151 **denunciation** proclamation of banns by the church. 153 **propagation** in-
crease. 154 **friends** kinsfolk. 161 **fault . . . newness** N. 166 **place**
office. 168 **stagger in** am in doubt about. 169 **the enrolled** read
'th' enrolled.' 170 **unscour'd** rusty. 171 **zodiacs . . . round** years
have passed. 172 **for a name** to acquire a reputation.

Now puts the drowsy and neglected act
Freshly on me: 'tis surely for a name. 174

Lucio. I warrant it is. And thy head stands so
tickle on thy shoulders that a milkmaid, if she be
in love, may sigh it off. Send after the Duke and
appeal to him.

Claudio. I have done so, but he's not to be found.
I prithee, Lucio, do me this kind service. 180
This day my sister should the cloister enter,
And there receive her approbation.
Acquaint her with the danger of my state,
Implore her, in my voice, that she make friends
To the strict deputy. Bid herself assay him— 185
I have great hope in that; for in her youth
There is a prone and speechless dialect,
Such as move men; beside, she hath prosperous **art**
When she will play with reason and discourse,
And well she can persuade. 190

Lucio. I pray she may: as well for the encourage-
ment of the like, which else would stand under grie-
vous imposition, as for the enjoying of thy life, who
I would be sorry should be thus foolishly lost at a
game of tick-tack. I'll to her. 195

Claudio. I thank you, good friend Lucio.

Lucio. Within two hours.

Claudio   Come, officer, away!
                                    Exeunt.

---

176 **tickle** unstable. 182 **receive her approbation** (five syllables
here) enter upon her novitiate. 184 **voice** name. 185 **assay** attempt, accost. 187 **prone** enticing. **prone and speechless dialect**
N. 188 **she hath prosperous** read 'she'th prosp'rous.' 195 **tick-
tack** a kind of backgammon in which pegs were fitted into
holes.

11

SCENE 3

Enter Duke and Friar Thomas.

Duke. No, holy Father, throw away that thought:
Believe not that the dribbling dart of love
Can pierce a complete bosom. Why I desire thee
To give me secret harbor hath a purpose   4
More grave and wrinkled than the aims and ends
Of burning youth.
    Friar.   May your Grace speak of it?
    Duke. My holy sir, none better knows than you
How I have ever lov'd the life remov'd
And held in idle price to haunt assemblies
Where youth and cost, witless bravery keeps.   10
I have deliver'd to Lord Angelo—
A man of stricture and firm abstinence—
My absolute power and place here in Vienna,
And he supposes me travel'd to Poland;
For so I have strew'd it in the common ear,   15
And so it is receiv'd. Now, pious sir,
You will demand of me why I do this?
    Friar. Gladly, my lord.
    Duke. We have strict statutes and most biting
    laws—   19
The needful bits and curbs to headstrong steeds—
Which for this fourteen years we have let slip;
Even like an oregrown lion in a cave,

2 **dribbling** feeble. 3 **complete** (stressed $\overset{\frown}{-}$ —) perfect. 9 **in idle price** as valueless. 10 **cost** extravagance. **bravery** ostentation. 12 **stricture** strictness. 15 **I have** read 'I've.' 17 **demand** ask. 20 **steeds** N. 21 **slip** N. 22 **Even** read 'E'en.' **oregrown** grown fat or old.

That goes not out to prey. Now, as fond fathers,
Having bound up the threat'ning twigs of birch,
Only to stick it in their children's sight   25
For terror, not to use, in time the rod
Becomes more mock'd than fear'd; so our decrees,
Dead to infliction, to themselves are dead,
And Liberty plucks Justice by the nose;
The baby beats the nurse, and quite athwart   30
Goes all decorum.
   Friar.   It rested in your Grace
To unloose this tied-up justice when you pleas'd;
And it in you more dreadful would have seem'd
Than in Lord Angelo.
   Duke.   I do fear, too dreadful:
Sith 'twas my fault to give the people scope,   35
'Twould be my tyranny to strike and gall them
For what I bid them do: for we bid this be done,
When evil deeds have their permissive pass
And not the punishment. Therefore, indeed, my
     Father,
I have on Angelo impos'd the office,   40
Who may, in th' ambush of my name, strike home,
And yet my nature never in the sight
To do it slander. And to behold his sway,
I will, as 'twere a brother of your order,   44
Visit both prince and people. Therefore, I prithee,
Supply me with the habit, and instruct me
How I may formally in person bear

23 **fond** foolish. 27 **Becomes** F omits. 28 **infliction** execution.
29 **Liberty** license. 32 **To unloose** read 't' unloose.' 35 **Sith** since.
36 **gall** hurt. 37–9 **for . . . punishment** N. 42–3 **And . . . slander**
N. 47 **bear** conduct myself.

Like a true friar. Moe reasons for this action
At our more leisure shall I render you;
Only this one: Lord Angelo is precise,   50
Stands at a guard with envy; scarce confesses
That his blood flows, or that his appetite
Is more to bread than stone. Hence shall we see,
If power change purpose, what our seemers be.

Exit [with Friar].

SCENE 4

Enter Isabel and Francisca, a Nun.

Isabella. And have you nuns no farther privileges?
Nun. Are not these large enough?
Isabella. Yes, truly. I speak not as desiring more,
But rather wishing a more strict restraint
Upon the sisterhood, the votarists of Saint Clare.   5

Lucio within.

Lucio. Ho! Peace be in this place!
Isabella.   Who's that which calls?
Nun. It is a man's voice. Gentle Isabella,
Turn you the key, and know his business of him.
You may, I may not. You are yet unsworn.   9
When you have vow'd, you must not speak with men
But in the presence of the prioress;
Then, if you speak, you must not show your face,
Or, if you show your face, you must not speak.
He calls again. I pray you, answer him.   [*Exit.*]
Isabella. Peace and prosperity! Who is't that calls?

48 **Moe** more. 49 **more** greater. 50 **precise** puritanical. 51 **Stands
. . . envy** guards against malice. 53 **to** inclined to.

[Enter Lucio.]

Lucio. Hail, virgin, if you be, as those cheek-roses
Proclaim you are no less! Can you so stead me
As bring me to the sight of Isabella,
A novice of this place, and the fair sister
To her unhappy brother, Claudio?   20
Isabella. Why 'her unhappy brother'? let me ask,
The rather for I now must make you know
I am that Isabella, and his sister.
Lucio. Gentle and fair, your brother kindly greets
    you.
Not to be weary with you, he's in prison.   25
Isabella. Woe me! for what?
Lucio. For that which, if myself might be his judge,
He should receive his punishment in thanks.
He hath got his friend with child.   29
Isabella. Sir, make me not your story.
Lucio.   'Tis true.
I would not, though 'tis my familiar sin
With maids to seem the lapwing and to jest,
Tongue far from heart, play with all virgins so.
I hold you as a thing enskied and sainted,
By your renouncement an immortal spirit,   35
And to be talk'd with in sincerity,
As with a saint.
Isabella. You do blaspheme the good in mocking me.
Lucio. Do not believe it. Fewness and truth, 'tis
    thus:
Your brother and his lover have embrac'd.   40
As those that feed grow full, as blossoming time

17 **stead** help. 25 **weary** tedious. 29 **friend** sweetheart, mistress.
30 **make . . . story** tell me no tales. 32 **lapwing** N. 34 **enskied**
heavenly. 39 **Fewness and truth** briefly and truly.

That from the seedness the bare fallow brings
To teeming foison, even so her plenteous womb
Expresseth his full tilth and husbandry.
  Isabella. Someone with child by him? My cousin
    Juliet?   45
  Lucio. Is she your cousin?
  Isabella. Adoptedly, as schoolmaids change their
    names
By vain though apt affection.
  Lucio.   She it is.
  Isabella. O, let him marry her!
  Lucio.   This is the point.
The Duke is very strangely gone from hence;   50
Bore many gentlemen—myself being one—
In hand and hope of action; but we do learn
By those that know the very nerves of state,
His givings-out were of an infinite distance
From his true-meant design. Upon his place,   55
And with full line of his authority,
Governs Lord Angelo, a man whose blood
Is very snow-broth; one who never feels
The wanton stings and motions of the sense
But doth rebate and blunt his natural edge   60
With profits of the mind, study and fast.
He—to give fear to use and liberty,
Which have for long run by the hideous law,
As mice by lions—hath pick'd out an act,
Under whose heavy sense your brother's life   65
Falls into forfeit; he arrests him on it,

42 **seedness** seeding. 43 **foison** rich harvest. 43 **even** read 'e'en.'
44 **tilth** tillage. 49 **marry** N. 51–2 **Bore . . . in hand** kept them
in expectation. 53 **nerves** sinews. 54 **givings-out** announced plans;
F *giving-out*. 56 **line** scope. 58 **snow-broth** melting snow. 59 **motions** impulses. **sense** sexual desire. 60 **rebate** dull. 62 **use and
liberty** licentious custom.

And follows close the rigor of the statute,
To make him an example. All hope is gone,
Unless you have the grace by your fair prayer   69
To soften Angelo. And that's my pith of business
'Twixt you and your poor brother.
  Isabella. Doth he so seek his life?
  Lucio.   Has censur'd him
Already and, as I hear, the provost hath
A warrant for his execution.
  Isabella. Alas! What poor ability's in me   75
To do him good?
  Lucio.   Assay the power you have.
  Isabella. My power? Alas! I doubt—
  Lucio.   Our doubts are traitors,
And make us lose the good we oft might win,
By fearing to attempt. Go to Lord Angelo,
And let him learn to know, when maidens sue,   80
Men give like gods; but when they weep and kneel,
All their petitions are as freely theirs
As they themselves would owe them.
  Isabella. I'll see what I can do.
  Lucio.   But speedily.
  Isabella. I will about it straight,   85
No longer staying but to give the Mother
Notice of my affair. I humbly thank you.
Commend me to my brother. Soon at night
I'll send him certain word of my success.   89
  Lucio. I take my leave of you.
  Isabella.   Good sir, adieu. *Exeunt.*

72–6 **Doth . . . have** N. 72 **censur'd** sentenced. 74 **execution** five syllables here. 78 **make** F *makes.* 82 **as freely theirs** as freely granted them. 83 **owe** possess. 86 **Mother** the abbess or prioress. 88 **Soon at night** early tonight. 89 **success** the consequence, good or bad.

Act II

SCENE 1

Enter Angelo, Escalus, and Servants, Justice.

Angelo. We must not make a scarecrow of the law,
Setting it up to fear the birds of prey,
And let it keep one shape, till custom make it
Their perch and not their terror.

Escalus.   Ay, but yet
Let us be keen and rather cut a little,   5
Than fall and bruise to death. Alas! This gentleman,
Whom I would save, had a most noble father.
Let but your Honor know—
Whom I believe to be most strait in virtue—
That, in the working of your own affections,   10
Had time coher'd with place or place with wishing,
Or that the resolute acting of your blood
Could have attain'd th' effect of your own purpose,
Whether you had not sometime in your life
Err'd in this point which now you censure him,   15
And pull'd the law upon you.

Angelo. 'Tis one thing to be tempted, Escalus,
Another thing to fall. I not deny,
The jury, passing on the prisoner's life,
May in the sworn twelve have a thief or two   20

2 **fear** frighten. 6 **fall** let fall, as an executioner's ax. 8 **know**
consider. 11 **coher'd** agreed. 12 **your** F *our.*

18

Guiltier than him they try; what's open made to
    justice,
That justice seizes: what knows the laws
That thieves do pass on thieves? 'Tis very pregnant
The jewel that we find, we stoop and tak't
Because we see it; but what we do not see   25
We tread upon, and never think of it.
You may not so extenuate his offense
For I have had such faults; but rather tell me,
When I, that censure him, do so offend,
Let mine own judgment pattern out my death,   30
And nothing come in partial. Sir, he must die.

Enter Provost.

Escalus. Be it as your wisdom will.
Angelo.   Where is the provost?
Provost. Here, if it like your Honor.
Angelo.   See that Claudio
Be executed by nine tomorrow morning:
Bring him his confessor, let him be prepar'd;   35
For that's the utmost of his pilgrimage.
                              [*Exit Provost.*]
Escalus. Well, heaven forgive him, and forgive us
    all!
Some rise by sin, and some by virtue fall:
Some run from brakes of vice, and answer none,
And some condemned for a fault alone.   40

Enter Elbow, Froth, Clown [Pompey], Officers.

Elbow. Come, bring them away. If these be good

22-3 what . . . thieves N. 23 pregnant evident. 28 For because.
31 come in partial intervene. 35 confessor stressed ´ — ´.
36 utmost of his pilgrimage limit of his earthly life. 39 brakes
of vice N. brakes thickets. vice F *ice.*

people in a commonweal that do nothing but use
their abuses in common houses, I know no law. Bring
them away.   44

Angelo. How now, sir! What's your name? And
what's the matter?

Elbow. If it please your Honor, I am the poor
Duke's constable, and my name is Elbow. I do lean
upon justice, sir, and do bring in here before your
good Honor two notorious benefactors.   50

Angelo. Benefactors! Well, what benefactors are
they? Are they not malefactors?

Elbow. If it please your Honor, I know not well
what they are; but precise villains they are, that I
am sure of, and void of all profanation in the world
that good Christians ought to have.   56

Escalus. This comes off well: here's a wise officer.

Angelo. Go to: what quality are they of? Elbow is
your name? Why dost thou not speak, Elbow?

Pompey. He cannot, sir. He's out at elbow.   60

Angelo. What are you, sir?

Elbow. He, sir! A tapster, sir; parcel-bawd; one
that serves a bad woman, whose house, sir, was, as
they say, pluck'd down in the suburbs; and now she
professes a hot-house, which I think is a very ill
house too.   66

Escalus. How know you that?

Elbow. My wife, sir, whom I detest before heaven
and your Honor—

Escalus. How! Thy wife?   70

43 **common houses** brothels. 54 **precise** precious, arrant. 55 **profanation** for 'profession.' 58 **quality** occupation. 62 **parcel-bawd**
part bawd, part tapster. 65 **hot-house** properly a bathhouse,
but commonly a brothel. 68 **detest** for 'protest' or 'attest.'

20

Elbow. Ay, sir; whom I thank heaven is an honest woman—

Escalus. Dost thou detest her therefore?

Elbow. I say, sir, I will detest myself also, as well as she, that this house, if it be not a bawd's house, it is pity of her life, for it is a naughty house. 76

Escalus. How dost thou know that, Constable?

Elbow. Marry, sir, by my wife; who, if she had bin a woman cardinally given, might have bin accus'd in fornication, adultery, and all uncleanliness there.

Escalus. By the woman's means? 81

Elbow. Ay, sir, by Mistress Overdone's means; but as she spit in his face, so she defied him.

Pompey. Sir, if it please your Honor, this is not so.

Elbow. Prove it before these varlets here, thou honorable man, prove it. 86

Escalus. Do you hear how he misplaces?

Pompey. Sir, she came in, great with child, and longing—saving your Honor's reverence—for stew'd prunes. Sir, we had but two in the house, which at that very distant time stood, as it were, in a fruit dish, a dish of some threepence; your Honors have seen such dishes; they are not China dishes, but very good dishes— 94

Escalus. Go to, go to: no matter for the dish, sir.

Pompey. No, indeed, sir, not of a pin; you are therein in the right: but to the point. As I say, this Mistress Elbow, being, as I say, with child, and being great-bellied, and longing, as I said, for prunes, and having but two in the dish, as I said, Master Froth here, this very man, having eaten the rest, as I said,

79 **cardinally** for 'carnally' and usually so pronounced. 87 **misplaces** i.e. words. 89–90 **stew'd prunes** N. 91 **distant** for 'instant.'

and, as I say, paying for them very honestly; for, as you know, Master Froth, I could not give you threepence again.

Froth. No, indeed. 105

Pompey. Very well: you being then, if you be rememb'red, cracking the stones of the foresaid prunes—

Froth. Ay, so I did, indeed. 109

Pompey. Why, very well: I telling you then, if you be rememb'red, that such a one and such a one were past cure of the thing you wot of, unless they kept very good diet, as I told you—

Froth. All this is true.

Pompey. Why, very well then— 115

Escalus. Come, you are a tedious fool: to the purpose. What was done to Elbow's wife, that he hath cause to complain of? Come me to what was done to her. 119

Pompey. Sir, your Honor cannot come to that yet.

Escalus. No, sir, nor I mean it not.

Pompey. Sir, but you shall come to it, by your Honor's leave. And I beseech you look into Master Froth here, sir: a man of fourscore pound a year, whose father died at Hallowmas. Was't not at Hallowmas, Master Froth? 126

Froth. Allhallond-Eve.

Pompey. Why very well: I hope here be truths. He, sir, sitting, as I say, in a lower chair, sir—'twas in the Bunch of Grapes, where indeed you have a delight to sit, have you not? 131

---

118 **Come me** come (*me* so-called ethical dative). 127 **Allhallond-Eve** Hallowe'en. 129 **lower** easy or reclining. 130 **Bunch of Grapes** N.

Froth. I have so, because it is an open room and good for winter.

Pompey. Why, very well then: I hope here be truths. 135

Angelo. This will last out a night in Russia,
When nights are longest there. I'll take my leave,
And leave you to the hearing of the cause,
Hoping you'll find good cause to whip them all.

Escalus. I think no less. Good morrow to your
Lordship. 140

Exit [*Angelo*].
Now, sir, come on: what was done to Elbow's wife, once more?

Pompey. Once, sir? There was nothing done to her once.

Elbow. I beseech you, sir, ask him what this man did to my wife. 146

Pompey. I beseech your Honor, ask me.

Escalus. Well, sir, what did this gentleman to her?

Pompey I beseech you, sir, look in this gentleman's face. Good Master Froth, look upon his Honor; 'tis for a good purpose. Doth your Honor mark his face?

Escalus. Ay, sir, very well.

Pompey. Nay, I beseech you, mark it well.

Escalus. Well, I do so. 154

Pompey. Doth your Honor see any harm in his face?

Escalus. Why, no.

Pompey. I'll be suppos'd upon a book, his face is the worst thing about him. Good, then: if his face be the worst thing about him, how could Master Froth do the constable's wife any harm? I would know that of your Honor.

132 **open** public. 158 **suppos'd** for 'deposed' (under oath).

23

Escalus. He's in the right. Constable, what say you to it? 164

Elbow. First, and it like you, the house is a respected house; next, this is a respected fellow; and his mistress is a respected woman.

Pompey. By this hand, sir, his wife is a more respected person than any of us all. 169

Elbow. Varlet, thou liest: thou liest, wicked varlet. The time is yet to come that she was ever respected with man, woman, or child.

Pompey. Sir, she was respected with him before he married with her. 174

Escalus. Which is the wiser here? Justice or Iniquity? Is this true?

Elbow. O thou caitiff! O thou varlet! O thou wicked Hannibal! I respected with her before I was married to her? If ever I was respected with her, or she with me, let not your Worship think me the poor Duke's officer. Prove this, thou wicked Hannibal, or I'll have my action of battery on thee.

Escalus. If he took you a box o' th' ear, you might have your action of slander, too. 184

Elbow. Marry, I thank your good Worship for it. What is't your Worship's pleasure I shall do with this wicked caitiff?

Escalus. Truly, officer, because he hath some offenses in him that thou wouldst discover if thou couldst, let him continue in his courses till thou know'st what they are.

Elbow. Marry, I thank your Worship for it. Thou seest, thou wicked varlet, now, what's come upon

165–6 respected for 'suspected.' 175–6 **Justice or Iniquity?** N. 178 **Hannibal,** for 'cannibal.' 183 **took** struck.

24

thee: thou art to continue now, thou varlet, thou art
to continue.   19½

Escalus. Where were you born, friend?

Froth. Here in Vienna, sir.

Escalus. Are you of fourscore pounds a year?

Froth. Yes, an't please you, sir.

Escalus. So. [*To Pompey.*] What trade are you of,
sir?   201

Pompey. A tapster, a poor widow's tapster.

Escalus. Your mistress' name?

Pompey. Mistress Overdone.   204

Escalus. Hath she had any more than one husband?

Pompey. Nine, sir; Overdone by the last.

Escalus. Nine! Come hither to me, Master Froth.
Master Froth, I would not have you acquainted with
tapsters; they will draw you, Master Froth, and
you will hang them. Get you gone, and let me hear
no more of you.

Froth. I thank your Worship. For mine own part,
I never come into any room in a taphouse, but I am
drawn in.   214

Escalus. Well, no more of it, Master Froth. Fare-
well.   [*Exit Froth.*]
Come you hither to me, Master tapster. What's your
name, Master tapster?

Pompey. Pompey.

Escalus. What else?   220

Pompey. Bum, sir.

Escalus. Troth, and your bum is the greatest thing
about you so that, in the beastliest sense, you are
Pompey the Great. Pompey, you are partly a bawd,
Pompey, howsoever you color it in being a tapster,

209 **draw you** N. 222 **bum** N.

are you not? Come, tell me true: it shall be the better for you.

Pompey. Truly, sir, I am a poor fellow that would live. 229

Escalus. How would you live, Pompey? By being a bawd? What do you think of the trade, Pompey? Is it a lawful trade?

Pompey. If the law would allow it, sir.

Escalus. But the law will not allow it, Pompey; nor it shall not be allowed in Vienna. 235

Pompey. Does your Worship mean to geld and splay all the youth of the city?

Escalus. No, Pompey.

Pompey. Truly, sir, in my poor opinion, they will to't then. If your Worship will take order for the drabs and the knaves, you need not to fear the bawds.

Escalus. There is pretty orders beginning, I can tell you: it is but heading and hanging. 244

Pompey. If you head and hang all that offend that way but for ten year together, you'll be glad to give out a commission for more heads. If this law hold in Vienna ten year, I'll rent the fairest house in it after threepence a bay. If you live to see this come to pass, say Pompey told you so. 250

Escalus. Thank you, good Pompey; and, in requital of your prophecy, hark you: I advise you, let me not find you before me again upon any complaint whatsoever; no, not for dwelling where you do. If I do, Pompey, I shall beat you to your tent, and prove a shrewd Caesar to you. In plain dealing, Pompey, I

236 geld castrate. 237 splay spay. 240 take order take measures. 241 drabs whores. 244 heading beheading. 249 after at the rate of. bay N. 255-6 I shall . . . you N.

26

shall have you whipt. So, for this time, Pompey, fare
you well. 258

Pompey. I thank your Worship for your good
counsel. [*Aside.*] But I shall follow it as the flesh
and fortune shall better determine.

Whip me! No, no, let carman whip his jade.

The valiant heart's not whipt out of his trade.

Exit.

Escalus. Come hither to me, Master Elbow; come
hither, Master Constable. How long have you been
in this place of constable? 266

Elbow. Seven year and a half, sir.

Escalus. I thought, by the readiness in the office,
you had continued in it some time. You say, seven
years together? 270

Elbow. And a half, sir.

Escalus. Alas, it hath been great pains to you!
They do you wrong to put you so oft upon't. Are
there not men in your ward sufficient to serve it?

Elbow. Faith, sir, few of any wit in such matters.
As they are chosen, they are glad to choose me for
them. I do it for some piece of money, and go through
with all.

Escalus. Look you bring me in the names of some
six or seven, the most sufficient of your parish. 280

Elbow. To your Worship's house, sir?

Escalus. To my house. Fare you well.

[*Exit Elbow.*]

What's o'clock, think you?

Justice. Eleven, sir.

Escalus. I pray you home to dinner with me. 285

Justice. I humbly thank you.

262 **carman** teamster. **jade** poor-spirited horse. 273 put . . .
upon't impose the office . . . upon you N. 274, 280 **sufficient** able.

Escalus. It grieves me for the death of Claudio.
But there's no remedy.

Justice. Lord Angelo is severe.

Escalus.   It is but needful.
Mercy is not itself, that oft looks so;   290
Pardon is still the nurse of second woe.
But yet poor Claudio! There is no remedy.
Come, sir.   *Exeunt.*

SCENE 2

Enter Provost, [and a] Servant.

Servant. He's hearing of a cause. He will come
    straight.
I'll tell him of you.

Provost.   Pray you, do. [*Exit Servant.*] I'll know
His pleasure; maybe he will relent. Alas!
He hath but as offended in a dream.
All sects, all ages smack of this vice—and he   5
To die for't!

Enter Angelo.

Angelo. Now, what's the matter, Provost?

Provost. Is it your will Claudio shall die tomorrow?

Angelo. Did I not tell thee, yea? Hadst thou not
    order?
Why dost thou ask again?

Provost.   Lest I might be too rash.
Under your good correction, I have seen,   10

291 still always. 5 sects classes of people. 10 Under . . . correction begging your pardon.

28

When, after execution, Judgment hath
Repented o'er his doom.
   Angelo.   Go to: let that be mine.
Do you your office, or give up your place,
And you shall well be spar'd.
   Provost.   I crave your Honor's pardon.
What shall be done, sir, with the groaning Juliet?
She's very near her hour.
   Angelo.   Dispose of her   16
To some more fitter place; and that with speed.

[*Enter Servant.*]

   Servant. Here is the sister of the man condemn'd
Desires access to you.
   Angelo.   Hath he a sister?   19
   Provost. Ay, my good lord, a very virtuous maid,
And to be shortly of a sisterhood,
If not already.
   Angelo.   Well, let her be admitted.
                         [*Exit Servant.*]
See you the fornicatress be remov'd.
Let her have needful, but not lavish, means;
There shall be order for't.

Enter Lucio and Isabella.

   Provost.   'Save your Honor!   25
   Angelo. Stay a little while. [*To Isabella.*] Y' are
welcome: what's your will?
   Isabella. I am a woeful suitor to your Honor,   29
Please but your Honor hear me.
   Angelo.   Well: what's your suit?
   Isabella. There is a vice that most I do abhor,
And most desire should meet the blow of justice,   30

For which I would not plead, but that I must;
For which I must not plead, but that I am
At war 'twixt will and will not.
   Angelo.   Well: the matter?
   Isabella. I have a brother is condemn'd to die.
I do beseech you, let it be his fault,   35
And not my brother.
   Provost. [*Aside*.] Heaven give thee moving graces!
   Angelo. Condemn the fault, and not the actor of
     it?
Why, every fault's condemn'd ere it be done.
Mine were the very cipher of a function,
To fine the faults whose fine stands in record,   40
And let go by the actor.
   Isabella.   O just, but severe law!
I had a brother then. Heaven keep your Honor!
   Lucio. [*Aside to Isabella*.] Give't not o'er so: to
    him again, entreat him,
Kneel down before him, hang upon his gown;
You are too cold. If you should need a pin,   45
You could not with more tame a tongue desire it.
To him, I say!
   Isabella. Must he needs die?
   Angelo.   Maiden, no remedy.
   Isabella. Yes: I do think that you might pardon
    him,   49
And neither heaven nor man grieve at the mercy.
   Angelo. I will not do't.
   Isabella.   But can you, if you would?
   Angelo. Look, what I will not, that I cannot do.
   Isabella. But might you do't, and do the world no
    wrong,

35–6 let . . . brother let the fault die and not my brother.
39 cipher zero, a mere nothing. 40–1 To fine . . . actor N. 40
record stressed — $\stackrel{\prime}{-}$. 46 tame spiritless.

If so your heart were touch'd with that remorse
As mine is to him!

Angelo. He's sentenc'd: 'tis too late. 55

Lucio. [*Aside to Isabella.*]   You are too cold.

Isabella. Too late? Why, no: I that do speak a
    word,
May call it back again. Well, believe this,
No ceremony that to great ones 'longs,
Not the king's crown, nor the deputed sword, 60
The marchal's truncheon, nor the judge's robe,
Become them with one half so good a grace
As mercy does.
If he had been as you, and you as he, 64
You would have slipp'd like him; but he, like you,
Would not have been so stern.

Angelo.   Pray you, be gone.

Isabella. I would to heaven I had your potency,
And you were Isabel! Should it then be thus?
No: I would tell what 'twere to be a judge,
And what a prisoner.

Lucio. [*Aside to Isabella.*] Ay, touch him; there's
    the vein. 70

Angelo. Your brother is a forfeit of the law,
And you but waste your words.

Isabella.   Alas, alas.
Why, all the souls that were were forfeit once,
And He that might the vantage best have took,
Found out the remedy. How would you be, 75
If He, which is the top of judgment, should

54 remorse pity. 58 back, not in F. 59 ceremony symbol of greatness. 'longs belongs. 61 truncheon staff of office. 67 potency power.
74 vantage advantage (to punish mankind). 76 top of judgment
supreme judge.

31

But judge you as you are? O think on that!
And mercy then will breathe within your lips,
Like man new made.

    Angelo.   Be you content, fair maid.
It is the law, not I, condemn your brother.   80
Were he my kinsman, brother or my son,
It should be thus with him: he must die tomorrow.

    Isabella. Tomorrow? O, that's sudden,
Spare him, spare him!   84
He's not prepar'd for death. Even for our kitchens
We kill the fowl of season. Shall we serve heaven
With less respect than we do minister
To our gross selves? Good, good my lord, bethink
    you:
Who is it that hath died for this offence?
There's many have committed it.

    Lucio.   [*Aside to Isabella.*] Ay, well said.

    Angelo. The law hath not been dead, though it hath
    slept.   91
Those many had not dar'd to do that evil,
If the first that did th' edict infringe
Had answer'd for his deed. Now 'tis awake,
Takes note of what is done, and like a prophet   95
Looks in a glass that shows what future evils,
Either new, or by remissness new-conceiv'd,
And so in progress to be hatch'd and born,
Are now to have no successive degrees,
But, ere they live, to end.

    Isabella.   Yet show some pity.   100

---

79 **new made** regenerate, hence in his original innocence. 85 **Even**
read 'E'en.' 86 **of season** when it is in season. 93 **edict** stressed
— ⌣. 96 **glass** crystal glass, of the kind used in divination. 97 **new**
F *now.* 99 **successive** (stressed ⌣ — ⌣) **degrees** descendants.
100 **ere** F *here.*

    32

Angelo. I show it most of all when I show justice,
For then I pity those I do not know,
Which a dismiss'd offense would after gall,
And do him right that, answering one foul wrong,
Lives not to act another. Be satisfied.   105
Your brother dies tomorrow. Be content.
  Isabella. So you must be the first that gives this
            sentence,
And he, that suffers. O, it is excellent
To have a giant's strength, but it is tyrannous
To use it like a giant!
  Lucio. [*Aside to Isabella.*] That's well said.   110
  Isabella. Could great men thunder
As Jove himself does, Jove would nere be quiet,
For every pelting, petty officer
Would use his heaven for thunder,
Nothing but thunder! Merciful heaven!   115
Thou rather with thy sharp and sulphurous bolt
Splits the unwedgeable and gnarled oak
Than the soft myrtle; but man, proud man,
Dress'd in a little brief authority,
Most ignorant of what he's most assur'd—   120
His glassy essence—like an angry ape,
Plays such fantastic tricks before high heaven
As makes the angels weep; who, with our spleens,
Would all themselves laugh mortal.
  Lucio. [*Aside to Isabella.*] O, to him, to him, wench!
            He will relent.   125
He's coming. I perceive't.

112. **nere** never. 113 **pelting** paltry. 117 **Splits** splitst. **unwedge-able** not to be split even with wedges. 121 **glassy essence** fragile being. 123 **spleens** the spleen was the organ once regarded as the seat of the emotions. 124 **laugh mortal** laugh themselves to death. 126 **coming** on the verge of relenting.

Provost. [*Aside.*]   Pray heaven she win him!

Isabella. We cannot weigh our brother with ourself:
Great men may jest with saints: 'tis wit in them,
But in the less foul profanation.

Lucio. [*Aside to Isabella.*] Thou'rt i' th' right,
    girl: more o' that.   130

Isabella. That in the captain's but a choleric word,
Which in the soldier is flat blasphemy.

Lucio [*Aside to Isabella.*] Art avis'd o' that? More
    on't.

Angelo. Why do you put these sayings upon me?

Isabella. Because Authority, though it err like
    others,   135
Hath yet a kind of medicine in itself,
That skins the vice o' th' top. Go to your bosom:
Knock there, and ask your heart what it doth know
That's like my brother's fault. If it confess
A natural guiltiness such as is his,   140
Let it not sound a thought upon your tongue
Against my brother's life.

Angelo. [*Aside.*]   She speaks, and 'tis
Such sense that my sense breeds with it. [*Aloud.*]
    Fare you well.

Isabella. Gentle my lord, turn back.   144

Angelo. I will bethink me. Come again tomorrow.

Isabella. Hark how I'll bribe you. Good my lord,
    turn back.

Angelo. How! Bribe me?

Isabella. Ay, with such gifts that heaven shall share
    with you.

127 **weigh . . . ourself** judge others by ourselves. 129 **less** lesser
men. 133 **avis'd** informed. 137 **skins** covers the sore without heal-
ing it. 140 **natural** read 'nat'ral.' 142–3 **She . . . it** N.

Lucio. [*Aside to Isabella.*] You had marr'd all else.

Isabella. Not with fond sickles of the tested gold,
Or stones whose rates are either rich or poor   151
As fancy values them; but with true prayers
That shall be up at heaven and enter there
Ere sunrise: prayers from preserved souls,
From fasting maids whose minds are dedicate   155
To nothing temporal.

Angelo.   Well: come to me tomorrow.

Lucio. [*Aside to Isabella.*] Go to: 'tis well. Away!

Isabella. Heaven keep your Honor safe!

Angelo. [*Aside.*]   Amen.
For I am that way going to temptation,
Where prayers cross.

Isabella.   At what hour tomorrow   160
Shall I attend your lordship?

Angelo.   At any time 'fore noon.

Isabella. 'Save your Honor!

        [*Exeunt Isabella, Lucio, and Provost.*]

Angelo.   From thee: even from
        thy virtue.
What's this? What's this? Is this her fault or mine?
The tempter, or the tempted, who sins most?
Ha!   165
Not she; nor doth she tempt. But it is I
That, lying by the violet in the sun,
Do as the carrion does, not as the flower,
Corrupt with virtuous season. Can it be
That modesty may more betray our sense   170
Than woman's lightness? Having waste ground
        enough,

150 sickles shekels. 151 rates F *rate.* 160 prayers cross N. 162
'Save God save. 169 Corrupt . . . season N. 170 sense sensu-
ality. 171 lightness wantonness.

35

Shall we desire to raze the sanctuary,
And pitch our evils there? O, fie, fie, fie!
What dost thou? Or what art thou, Angelo?
Dost thou desire her foully for those things   175
That make her good? O, let her brother live!
Thieves for their robbery have authority
When judges steal themselves. What! do I love her,
That I desire to hear her speak again,
And feast upon her eyes? What is't I dream on?   180
O cunning enemy that, to catch a saint,
With saints dost bait thy hook! Most dangerous
Is that temptation that doth goad us on
To sin in loving virtue. Never could the strumpet,
With all her double vigor, art and nature,   185
Once stir my temper; but this virtuous maid
Subdues me quite. Ever till now,
When men were fond, I smil'd and wonder'd how.
                                                Exit.

SCENE 3

Enter Duke [disguised as a friar] and Provost.

Duke. Hail to you, Provost! So I think you are.
Provost. I am the provost. What's your will, good
    Friar?
Duke. Bound by my charity and my bless'd order,
I come to visit the afflicted spirits
Here in the prison. Do me the common right   5
To let me see them and to make me know
The nature of their crimes, that I may minister
To them accordingly.

173 evils N. 188 fond doting. 1 So such.
36

Provost. I would do more than that, if more were
needful.

Enter Julietta.

Look, here comes one: a gentlewoman of mine,　　10
Who, falling in the flames of her own youth,
Hath blister'd her report. She is with child,
And he that got it, sentenc'd: a young man
More fit to do another such offense,
Than die for this.　　　　　　　　　　　　15
　Duke. When must he die?
　Provost.　　　　　As I do think, tomorrow.
[*To Julietta.*] I have provided for you. Stay a while,
And you shall be conducted.
　Duke. Repent you, fair one, of the sin you carry?
　Julietta. I do, and bear the shame most patiently.
　Duke. I'll teach you how you shall arraign your
　　conscience,　　　　　　　　　　　　　21
And try your penitence, if it be sound,
Or hollowly put on.
　Julietta.　　　　I'll gladly learn.
　Duke. Love you the man that wrong'd you?
　Julietta. Yes, as I love the woman that wrong'd
　　him.　　　　　　　　　　　　　　　25
　Duke. So then it seems your most offenseful act
Was mutually committed?
　Julietta.　　　　Mutually.
　Duke. Then was your sin of heavier kind than his.
　Julietta. I do confess it, and repent it, Father.
　Duke. 'Tis meet so, daughter: but lest you do re-
　　pent,　　　　　　　　　　　　　　30
As that the sin hath brought you to this shame,

11 flames F *flawes.* 12 blister'd her report besmirched her
reputation. 23 hollowly insincerely. 30 meet proper.

Which sorrow is always toward ourselves, not heaven,
Showing we would not spare heaven as we love it,
But as we stand in fear—
  Julietta. I do repent me, as it is an evil,   35
And take the shame with joy.
  Duke.   There rest.
Your partner, as I hear, must die tomorrow,
And I am going with instruction to him.
Grace go with you, *Benedicite.*   *Exit.*
  Julietta. Must die tomorrow! O injurious love,   40
That respites me a life, whose very comfort
Is still a dying horror!
  Provost.   'Tis pity of him.   *Exeunt.*

SCENE 4

Enter Angelo.

  Angelo. When I would pray and think, I think and
        pray
To several subjects. Heaven hath my empty words,
Whilst my invention, hearing not my tongue,
Anchors on Isabel: heaven in my mouth,
As if I did but only chew his name,   5
And in my heart the strong and swelling evil
Of my conception. The state, whereon I studied,
Is like a good thing, being often read,
Grown sear'd and tedious; yea, my gravity,
Wherein, let no man hear me, I take pride,   10

32 sorrow is read 'sorrow's.' 33 spare heaven as refrain from
offending heaven because. 40–2 O . . . horror N. 2 several different. 3 invention imagination. 7 conception thought. 9 sear'd
dry; F *feard.*

Could I, with boot, change for an idle plume,
Which the air beats for vain. O place! O form!
How often dost thou with thy case, thy habit,
Wrench awe from fools, and tie the wiser souls
To thy false seeming! Blood, thou art blood: 15
Let's write 'good Angel' on the devil's horn,
Is't not the devil's crest? How now! who's there?

Enter Servant.

Servant. One Isabel, a sister, desires access to you.
Angelo. Teach her the way. [*Exit Servant.*] O
heavens!
Why does my blood thus muster to my heart, 20
Making both it unable for itself,
And dispossessing all my other parts
Of necessary fitness?
So play the foolish throngs with one that swounds:
Come all to help him, and so stop the air 25
By which he should revive; and even so
The general, subject to a well-wish'd king,
Quit their own part, and in obsequious fondness
Crowd to his presence, where their untaught love
Must needs appear offense.

Enter Isabella.

How now, fair maid! 30
Isabella. I am come to know your pleasure.
Angelo. That you might know it, would much better
please me

11 boot advantage. plume a feather or panache, emblematic of
frivolity. 12 vain quibble on 'vane.' 13 case external show. habit
dress. 16-17 Let's write . . . crest N. 21 unable weak. 24
swounds swoons. 27 general common people. 28 obsequious duti-
ful. 32 know N.

Than to demand what 'tis. Your brother cannot live.

Isabella. Even so. Heaven keep your Honor!

Angelo. Yet may he live a while; and, it may be, 35
As long as you or I. Yet he must die.

Isabella. Under your sentence?

Angelo. Yea.

Isabella. When, I beseech you? that in his reprieve,
Longer or shorter, he may be so fitted 40
That his soul sicken not.

Angelo. Ha! fie, these filthy vices! It were as good
To pardon him that hath from nature stolne
A man already made, as to remit 44
Their saucy sweetness that do coin heaven's image
In stamps that are forbid: 'tis all as easy
Falsely to take away a life true made,
As to put metal in restrained meanes
To make a false one.

Isabella. 'Tis set down so in heaven, but not in
earth. 50

Angelo. Say you so? Then I shall pose you quickly.
Which had you rather, that the most just law
Now took your brother's life; or, to redeem him,
Give up your body to such sweet uncleanness
As she that he hath stain'd?

Isabella. Sir, believe this, 55
I had rather give my body than my soul.

Angelo. I talk not of your soul. Our compell'd sins

40 **fitted** prepared for death. 43 **stolne** stolen. 44 **remit** pardon.
45 **saucy** lascivious. 46 **stamps** dies for making coins. **all** quite.
46-9 **'tis . . . one** N. 47 **Falsely** illegally. 48 **restrained** forbidden. **meanes** mints. 50 **'Tis . . . earth** N. 51 **pose you** put a hard question to you. 56 **I had** read 'I'd.' 57 **compell'd** stressed — —.

Stand more for number than for accompt.

Isabella. How say
you?

Angelo. Nay, I'll not warrant that; for I can speak
Against the thing I say. Answer to this: 60
I, now the voice of the recorded law,
Pronounce a sentence on your brother's life.
Might there not be a charity in sin
To save this brother's life?

Isabella. Please you to do't,
I'll take it as a peril to my soul. 65
It is no sin at all, but charity.

Angelo. Pleas'd you to do't, at peril of your soul,
Were equal poise of sin and charity.

Isabella. That I do beg his life, if it be sin,
Heaven let me bear it! You granting of my suit, 70
If that be sin, I'll make it my morn prayer
To have it added to the faults of mine
And nothing of your answer.

Angelo. Nay, but hear me.
Your sense pursues not mine: either you are igno-
rant,
Or seem so craftily; and that's not good. 75

Isabella. Let me be ignorant, and in nothing good,
But graciously to know I am no better.

Angelo. Thus wisdom wishes to appear most bright
When it doth tax itself, as these black masks
Proclaim an enshield beauty ten times louder 80
Than beauty could, display'd. But mark me.
To be received plain, I'll speak more gross:

58 **for accompt** (pronounced 'account') N. 59 **that** i.e. Angelo's
argument in ll. 57–8. 73 **nothing of your answer** nothing for which
you can be held accountable. 75 **craftily** F *crafty*. 76 **me** F omits
79 **tax** reprove. 80 **enshield** concealed N. 82 **gross** plainly.

41

Your brother is to die.

Isabella. So.

Angelo. And his offense is so, as it appears,   85
Accountant to the law upon that pain.

Isabella. True.

Angelo. Admit no other way to save his life—
As I subscribe not that, nor any other,
But in the loss of question—that you, his sister,   90
Finding yourself desir'd of such a person,
Whose credit with the judge, or own great place,
Could fetch your brother from the manacles
Of the all-building law; and that there were
No earthly mean to save him, but that either   95
You must lay down the treasures of your body
To this suppos'd, or else to let him suffer,
What would you do?

Isabella. As much for my poor brother as myself:
That is, were I under the terms of death,   100
Th' impression of keen whips I'ld wear as rubies,
And strip myself to death, as to a bed
That longing have been sick for, ere I'ld yield
My body up to shame.

Angelo.   Then must your brother die.

Isabella. And 'twere the cheaper way: 105
Better it were a brother died at once,
Than that a sister, by redeeming him,
Should die for ever.

Angelo. Were not you then as cruel as the sentence
That you have slander'd so?   110

86 **pain** punishment. 89 **subscribe** admit. 90 **in . . . question** in
idle conversation (?). 92 **place** official position. 94 **all-building**
upon which all is founded. 95 **mean** means. 103 **have I** have.

Isabella. Ignomy in ransom and free pardon
Are of two houses: lawful mercy
Is nothing kin to foul redemption.

  Angelo. You seem'd of late to make the law a ty-
    rant,
And rather prov'd the sliding of your brother   115
A merriment than a vice.

  Isabella. O, pardon me, my lord! It oft falls out,
To have what we would have, we speak not what we
    mean.
I something do excuse the thing I hate,
For his advantage that I dearly love.   120

  Angelo. We are all frail.

  Isabella.   Else let my brother die,
If not a fedary, but only he
Owe and succeed thy weakness.

  Angelo. Nay, women are frail too.

  Isabella. Ay, as the glasses where they view them-
    selves,   125
Which are as easy broke as they make forms.
Women! Help heaven! Men their creation mar
In profiting by them. Nay, call us ten times frail,
For we are soft as our complexions are,
And credulous to false prints.

  Angelo.   I think it well: 130
And from this testimony of your own sex—
Since I suppose we are made to be no stronger
Than faults may shake our frames—let me be bold.
I do arrest your words. Be that you are,

111 Ignomy ignominy. 115 sliding backsliding. 122-3 If . . .
weakness N. 122 fedary associate. 123 owe possess. succeed
inherit. 126 forms images, reflections. 127-8 Men . . . them N.
130 credulous susceptible. prints impressions. 134 I . . . words
I take them as security.

That is, a woman; if you be more, you're none.   135
If you be one, as you are well express'd
By all external warrants, show it now,
By putting on the destin'd livery.

  Isabella. I have no tongue but one. Gentle my lord,
Let me entreat you speak the former language.   140

  Angelo. Plainly conceive, I love you.

  Isabella. My brother did love Juliet.
And you tell me that he shall die for't.

  Angelo. He shall not, Isabel, if you give me love.

  Isabella. I know your virtue hath a licence in't,   145
Which seems a little fouler than it is,
To pluck on others.

  Angelo.   Believe me, on mine honor,
My words express my purpose.

  Isabella. Ha! little honor to be much believ'd
And most pernicious purpose! Seeming, seeming!   150
I will proclaim thee, Angelo; look for't!
Sign me a present pardon for my brother,
Or with an outstretch'd throat I'll tell the world
    aloud
What man thou art.

  Angelo.   Who will believe thee, Isabel?
My unsoil'd name, th' austereness of my life,   155
My vouch against you, and my place i' th' state,
Will so your accusation overweigh,
That you shall stifle in your own report
And smell of calumny. I have begun,
And now I give my sensual race the rein.   160
Fit thy consent to my sharp appetite;

138 **destin'd livery** i.e. the frailty of your sex. 139 **tongue** language. 140 **former language** i.e. the unambiguous language employed earlier. 145–7 **I . . . others** N. 156 **vouch** testimony. 160 **race** nature, with a quibble.

Lay by all nicety and prolixious blushes,
That banish what they sue for: redeem thy brother
By yielding up thy body to my will,
Or else he must not only die the death,   165
But thy unkindness shall his death draw out
To ling'ring sufferance. Answer me tomorrow,
Or, by the affection that now guides me most,
I'll prove a tyrant to him. As for you,   169
Say what you can, my false oreweighs your true.

Exit.

  Isabella. To whom should I complain? Did I tell
    this,
Who would believe me? O perilous mouths!
That bear in them one and the selfsame tongue,
Either of condemnation or approof,
Bidding the law make curtsy to their will,   175
Hooking both right and wrong to th' appetite,
To follow as it draws. I'll to my brother.
Though he hath falne by prompture of the blood,
Yet hath he in him such a mind of honor,
That, had he twenty heads to tender down   180
On twenty bloody blocks, he'd yield them up,
Before his sister should her body stoop
To such abhorr'd pollution.
Then, Isabel, live chaste, and, brother, die:
More than our brother is our chastity.   185
I'll tell him yet of Angelo's request,
And fit his mind to death, for his soul's rest.   *Exit.*

162 **nicety** coyness, reserve. **prolixious** superfluous. 167 **suf-ferance** pain. 168 **affection** lust. 174 **approof** approbation. 178 **falne** fallen. **prompture** instigation.

Act III

SCENE 1

Enter Duke [as a friar], Claudio, and Provost.

Duke. So then you hope of pardon from Lord Angelo?

Claudio. The miserable have no other medicine
But only hope:
I have hope to live, and am prepar'd to die.   4

Duke. Be absolute for death. Either death or life
Shall thereby be the sweeter. Reason thus with life:
If I do lose thee, I do lose a thing
That none but fools would keep. A breath thou **art**,
Servile to all the skyey influences,
That dost this habitation, where thou keep'st,   10
Hourly afflict. Merely, thou art Death's fool,
For him thou labor'st by thy flight to shun,
And yet run'st toward him still. Thou art not noble,
For all th' accommodations that thou bear'st   14
Are nurs'd by baseness. Thou'rt by no means valiant,
For thou dost fear the soft and tender fork
Of a poor worm. Thy best of rest is sleep,
And that thou oft provok'st; yet grossly fear'st
Thy death, which is no more. Thou art not thyself,
For thou exists on many a thousand grains   20
That issue out of dust. Happy thou art not;
For what thou hast not, still thou striv'st to get,

5 absolute wholly determined. 9 skyey influences N. 14–15 **For**
. . . baseness N. 16–17 **For** . . . worm N.

And what thou hast, forget'st. Thou art not certain,
For thy complexion shifts to strange effects,
After the moon. If thou art rich, thou'rt poor;   25
For, like an ass whose back with ingots bows,
Thou bear'st thy heavy riches but a journey,
And Death unloads thee. Friend hast thou none,
For thine own bowels, which do call thee sire,
The mere effusion of thy proper loins,   30
Do curse the gout, serpigo, and the rheum,
For ending thee no sooner. Thou hast nor youth nor
       age,
But, as it were, an after-dinner's sleep,
Dreaming on both; for all thy blessed youth
Becomes as aged, and doth beg the alms   35
Of palsied Eld: and when thou art old and rich,
Thou hast neither heat, affection, limb, nor beauty,
To make thy riches pleasant. What's yet in this
That bears the name of life? Yet in this life
Lie hid moe thousand deaths; yet death we fear,   40
That makes these odds all even.

 Claudio.   I humbly thank you.
To sue to live, I find I seek to die,
And, seeking death, find life: let it come on.

Enter Isabella.

Isabella. What, ho! Peace here. Grace and good
 company!
Provost. Who's there? Come in, the wish deserves a
 welcome.   45

23 certain constant. 24–5 For . . . moon N. 29 bowels offspring.
30 effusion pouring-out. 31 serpigo spreading skin disease. F
Sapego. rheum excessive moisture in the body, causing catarrh.
32–4 Thou . . . both N. 34–6 for . . . Eld N. 36 thou art read
'thou'rt.' 37 limb vigor. 40 moe i.e. more than those mentioned.
SD Enter Isabella N.

Duke. Dear sir, ere long I'll visit you again.

Claudio. Most holy sir, I thank you.

Isabella. My business is a word or two with Claudio.

Provost. And very welcome. Look, Signior; here's
    your sister.

Duke. Provost, a word with you.   50

Provost. As many as you please.

Duke. Bring me to hear them speak, where I may
    be conceal'd.   [*Duke and Provost withdraw.*]

Claudio. Now, sister, what's the comfort?

Isabella. Why,   55
As all comforts are: most good, most good indeed.
Lord Angelo, having affairs to heaven,
Intends you for his swift ambassador,
Where you shall be an everlasting leiger.
Therefore, your best appointment make with speed;
Tomorrow you set on.

Claudio.   Is there no remedy?   61

Isabella. None but such remedy as, to save a head,
To cleave a heart in twain.

Claudio.   But is there any?

Isabella. Yes, brother, you may live.
There is a divelish mercy in the judge,   65
If you'll implore it, that will free your life,
But fetter you till death.

Claudio.   Perpetual durance?

Isabella. Ay, just—perpetual durance, a restraint,
Though all the world's vastidity you had,
To a determin'd scope.

Claudio.   But in what nature?   70

52 me to hear them F *them to hear me.* SD **Duke and Provost
withdraw** N. 59 **leiger** resident ambassador. 60 **appointment**
preparation. 65 **divelish** F devilish. 67 **durance** imprisonment.
68 **just** exactly. 69–70 **Though . . . scope** N. 69 **Though** F
through. **vastidity** immensity.

48

Isabella. In such a one as, you consenting to't,
Would bark your honor from that trunk you bear,
And leave you naked.

Claudio.   Let me know the point.

Isabella. O, I do fear thee, Claudio, and I quake,
Lest thou a feverous life shouldst entertain,   75
And six or seven winters more respect
Than a perpetual honor. Dar'st thou die?
The sense of death is most in apprehension,
And the poor beetle that we tread upon
In corporal sufferance finds a pang as great   80
As when a giant dies.

Claudio.   Why give you me this shame?
Think you I can a resolution fetch
From flow'ry tenderness? If I must die,
I will encounter darkness as a bride,
And hug it in mine arms.   85

Isabella. There spake my brother: there my father's
      grave
Did utter forth a voice. Yes, thou must die:
Thou art too noble to conserve a life
In base appliances. This outward-sainted deputy,
Whose settled visage and deliberate word   90
Nips youth i' th' head, and follies doth enew
As falcon doth the fowl, is yet a divel.
His filth within being cast, he would appear
A pond as deep as hell.

Claudio.   The prenzie Angelo!

---

72 **bark** strip. 75 **feverous** read 'fev'rous.' **entertain** maintain.
80 **corporal sufferance** read 'corp'ral suff'rance.' 80 **finds** experiences. 82 **a resolution fetch** derive courage. 89 **in base appliances**
by base means. 90 **settled** composed. 91 **enew** drive into the
water (a term from falconry). F *emmew.* 93 **cast** emptied, as a
pond of mud and refuse. 94 **prenzie** puritanical (?) N.

Isabella. O, 'tis the cunning livery of hell, 95
The damned'st body to invest and cover
In prenzie guards! Dost thou think, Claudio?
If I would yield him my virginity,
Thou mightst be freed.

Claudio.   O heavens! it cannot be.

Isabella. Yes, he would give't thee, from this rank
offense, 100
So to offend him still. This night's the time
That I should do what I abhor to name,
Or else thou diest tomorrow.

Claudio.   Thou shalt not do't.

Isabella. O! were it but my life,
I'd throw it down for your deliverance 105
As frankly as a pin.

Claudio.   Thanks, dear Isabel.

Isabella. Be ready, Claudio, for your death tomorrow.

Claudio. Yes. Has he affections in him,
That thus can make him bite the law by th' nose,
When he would force it: Sure it is no sin; 110
Or of the deadly seven it is the least.

Isabella. Which is the least?

Claudio. If it were damnable, he being so wise,
Why would he for the momentary trick 114
Be perdurably fin'd? O Isabel!

Isabella. What says my brother?

Claudio.   Death is a fearful
thing.

Isabella. And shamed life a hateful.

Claudio. Ay, but to die, and go we know not where,

97 guards trimmings. 101 still always. 108 affections passions.
109 bite by th' nose treat with contempt. 110 force enforce.
115 perdurably fin'd eternally punished.

To lie in cold obstruction and to rot,
This sensible warm motion to become   120
A kneaded clod; and the delighted spirit
To bathe in fiery floods, or to reside
In thrilling region of thick-ribbed ice,
To be imprison'd in the viewless winds,
And blown with restless violence round about   125
The pendent world; or to be worse than worst
Of those that lawless and incertain thought
Imagine howling: 'tis too horrible!
The weariest and most loathed worldly life
That age, ache, penury and imprisonment   130
Can lay on nature is a paradise
To what we fear of death.
  Isabella. Alas! alas!
  Claudio.   Sweet sister, let me live.
What sin you do to save a brother's life,
Nature dispenses with the deed so far   135
That it becomes a virtue.
  Isabella.   O you beast!
O faithless coward! O dishonest wretch!
Wilt thou be made a man out of my vice?
Is't not a kind of incest, to take life   139
From thine own sister's shame? What should I think?
Heaven shield my mother play'd my father fair,
For such a warped slip of wilderness
Nere issu'd from his blood. Take my defiance,
Die, perish! Might but my bending down
Reprieve thee from thy fate, it should proceed.   145
I'll pray a thousand prayers for thy death,

119 **obstruction** stagnation (of the blood). 121 **kneaded** i.e. like
dough. **delighted** accustomed to delight. 123 **thrilling** piercing
(with cold). **region** tract N. 124 **viewless** invisible. 135 dispenses
with pardons. 141 **shield** forbid. 142 **slip of wilderness** worthless
slip or scion. 145 **proceed** take place.

No word to save thee.

Claudio. Nay, hear me, Isabel.

Isabella.   O, fie, fie, fie!
Thy sin's not accidental, but a trade.
Mercy to thee would prove itself a bawd.   150
'Tis best that thou diest quickly.   [*Going.*]

Claudio.   O hear me, Isabella.
                              [*Duke comes forward.*]

Duke. Vouchsafe a word, young sister, but one word.

Isabella. What is your will?

Duke. Might you dispense with your leisure, I would
by and by have some speech with you: the satisfaction I would require is likewise your own benefit. 156

Isabella. I have no superfluous leisure: my stay
must be stolen out of other affairs; but I will attend
you a while.   159

Duke. [*Aside to Claudio.*] Son, I have overheard
what pass'd between you and your sister. Angelo had
never the purpose to corrupt her; only he hath made
an assay of her virtue to practice his judgment with
the disposition of natures. She, having the truth of
honor in her, hath made him that gracious denial
which he is most glad to receive. I am confessor to
Angelo, and I know this to be true; therefore prepare yourself to death. Do not satisfy your resolution with hopes that are fallible: tomorrow you must
die. Go to your knees and make ready.   170

Claudio. Let me ask my sister pardon. I am so out
of love with life that I will sue to be rid of it.

Duke. Hold you there: farewell.   [*Exit Claudio.*]

155 **by and by** immediately. 163 **practice his judgment** experi-
ment. 164 **disposition of natures** evaluation of character. 168-9
satisfy your resolution fortify your courage. 173 **Hold you there**
persist in that course.

[Enter Provost.]

Provost, a word with you.

Provost. What's your will, Father?   175

Duke. That now you are come, you will be gone.
Leave me a while with the maid. My mind promises
with my habit no loss shall touch her by my company.   179

Provost. In good time.   *Exit.*

Duke. The hand that hath made you fair hath made
you good. The goodness that is cheap in beauty
makes beauty brief in goodness; but grace, being the
soul of your complexion, shall keep the body of it
ever fair. The assault that Angelo hath made to you,
fortune hath convey'd to my understanding; and,
but that frailty hath examples for his falling, I
should wonder at Angelo. How will you do to content this substitute, and to save your brother?   189

Isabella. I am now going to resolve him. I had
rather my brother die by the law than my son should
be unlawfully born. But O, how much is the good
Duke deceived in Angelo! If ever he return and I
can speak to him, I will open my lips in vain, or discover his government.   195

Duke. That shall not be much amiss: yet, as the
matter now stands, he will avoid your accusation; he
made trial of you only. Therefore, fasten your ear on
my advisings: to the love I have in doing good a
remedy presents itself. I do make myself believe that
you may most uprighteously do a poor wronged lady
a merited benefit, redeem your brother from the an-

178 loss harm. 180 **In good time** well and good. 182 **cheap** lightly
esteemed. 185 **assault** love-proposal. 189 **substitute** i.e. Angelo.
190 **resolve** free from uncertainty. 194-5 **discover** reveal. 195
government conduct. 197 **avoid** make void, refute.

gry law, do no stain to your own gracious person, and much please the absent Duke, if peradventure he shall ever return to have hearing of this business.

Isabella. Let me hear you speak farther. I have spirit to do anything that appears not foul in the truth of my spirit. 208

Duke. Virtue is bold, and goodness never fearful. Have you not heard speak of Mariana, the sister of Frederick, the great soldier who miscarried at sea?

Isabella. I have heard of the lady, and good words went with her name. 213

Duke. She should this Angelo have married, was affianced to her by oath, and the nuptial appointed: between which time of the contract and limit of the solemnity, her brother Frederick was wrack'd at sea, having in that perished vessel the dowry of his sister. But mark how heavily this befell to the poor gentlewoman: there she lost a noble and renowned brother, in his love toward her ever most kind and natural; with him the portion and sinew of her fortune, her marriage dowry; with both, her combinate husband, this well-seeming Angelo. 224

Isabella. Can this be so? Did Angelo so leave her?

Duke. Left her in her tears, and dried not one of them with his comfort; swallowed his vows whole, pretending in her discoveries of dishonor: in few, bestowed her on her own lamentation, which she yet wears for his sake; and he, a marble to her tears, washed with them, but relents not. 231

Isabella. What a merit were it in death to take this

214–5 was affianced i.e. Angelo. 215 by F omits. 216–7 between . . . solemnity N. 223 combinate betrothed. 228 in few in a few words. 229 bestowed her on i.e. abandoned her to. 230 marble i.e. hard-hearted.

poor maid from the world! What corruption in this life, that it will let this man live! But how out of this can she avail? 235

Duke. It is a rupture that you may easily heal; and the cure of it not only saves your brother, but keeps you from dishonor in doing it.

Isabella. Show me how, good Father. 239

Duke. This forenamed maid hath yet in her the continuance of her first affection: his unjust unkindness, that in all reason should have quenched her love, hath, like an impediment in the current, made it more violent and unruly. Go you to Angelo: answer his requiring with a plausible obedience, agree with his demands to the point. Only refer yourself to this advantage: first, that your stay with him may not be long, that the time may have all shadow and silence in it, and the place answer to convenience. This being granted in course—and now follows all—we shall advise this wronged maid to stead up your appointment, go in your place. If the encounter acknowledge itself hereafter, it may compel him to her recompense; and here, by this is your brother saved, your honor untainted, the poor Mariana advantaged, and the corrupt deputy scaled. The maid will I frame and make fit for his attempt. If you think well to carry this, as you may, the doubleness of the benefit defends the deceit from reproof. What think you of it? 260

Isabella. The image of it gives me content already,

235 **avail** benefit. 245 **plausible** fair-seeming. 246 **refer yourself to** have recourse to. 248 **shadow** darkness. 250 **in course** as a matter of course. 251 **stead up** assume. 256 **scaled** weighed, as by scales. 257 **frame** instruct. 261 **image** mental picture.

and I trust it will grow to a most prosperous per-
fection.

Duke. It lies much in your holding up. Haste you
speedily to Angelo. If for this night he entreat you
to his bed, give him promise of satisfaction. I will
presently to St. Luke's; there, at the moated grange,
resides this dejected Mariana. At that place call
upon me, and dispatch with Angelo, that it may be
quickly. 270

Isabella. I thank you for this comfort. Fare you
well, good Father. *Exit.*

Enter Elbow, Clown [Pompey, and] Officers.

Elbow. Nay, if there be no remedy for it but that
you will needs buy and sell men and women like
beasts, we shall have all the world drink brown and
white bastard. 276

Duke. O heavens! What stuff is here?

Pompey. 'Twas never merry world, since, of two
usuries, the merriest was put down, and the worser
allow'd by order of law a furr'd gown to keep him
warm; and furr'd with fox and lamb skins too, to
signify that craft, being richer than innocency,
stands for the facing. 283

Elbow. Come your way, sir. Bless you, good Father
Friar.

Duke. And you, good brother father. What offense
hath this man made you, sir?

Elbow. Marry, sir, he hath offended the law; and,
sir, we take him to be a thief too, sir, for we have

267 **grange** a secluded country house. 268 **dejected** rejected, dis-
spirited. 269 **dispatch** come to an agreement. SD **Exit** N.
276 **bastard** a sweet Spanish wine. 278-9 **two usuries** N. 283
facing trimming. 286 **brother father** N.

found upon him, sir, a strange picklock, which we
have sent to the deputy.   291

Duke. Fie, sirrah! A bawd, a wicked bawd!
The evil that thou causest to be done,
That is thy means to live. Do thou but think
What 'tis to cram a maw or clothe a back   295
From such a filthy vice. Say to thyself,
From their abominable and beastly touches
I drink, I eat, array myself, and live.
Canst thou believe thy living is a life,
So stinkingly depending? Go mend, go mend.   300

Pompey. Indeed, it does stink in some sort, sir; but
yet, sir, I would prove—

Duke. Nay, if the divel have given thee proofs for
    sin,
Thou wilt prove his. Take him to prison, officer.
Correction and instruction must both work   305
Ere this rude beast will profit.

Elbow. He must before the deputy, sir; he has given
him warning. The deputy cannot abide a whoremas-
ter: if he be a whoremonger, and comes before him,
he were as good go a mile on his errand.   310

Duke. That we were all, as some would seem to be,
Free from our faults, as faults from seeming, free!

Enter Lucio.

Elbow. His neck will come to your waist—a cord,
sir.

Pompey. I spy comfort: I cry bail. Here's a gentleman and a friend of mine.   316

Lucio. How now, noble Pompey! What, at the

290 **picklock** skeleton key. 298 **array** F *away.* 300 **stinkingly
depending** depending upon such a stinking means of support.
310 **go . . . errand** i.e. give himself up for lost. 312 **Free** F omits.
313 **His . . . waist** N.

57

wheels of Caesar? Art thou led in triumph? What,
is there none of Pygmalion's images, newly made
woman, to be had now, for putting the hand in the
pocket and extracting it clutched? What reply? ha?
What say'st thou to this tune, matter and method?
Is't not drowned i' th' last rain, ha? What say'st
thou, Trot? Is the world as it was, man? Which is
the way? Is it sad, and few words, or how? The trick
of it?   326

Duke. Still thus, and thus, still worse!

Lucio. How doth my dear morsel, thy mistress?
Procures she still, ha?

Pompey. Troth, sir, she hath eaten up all her beef,
and she is herself in the tub.

Lucio. Why, 'tis good. It is the right of it; it must
be so. Ever your fresh whore and your powder'd
bawd: an unshunned consequence, it must be so. Art
going to prison, Pompey?   335

Pompey. Yes, faith, sir.

Lucio. Why, 'tis not amiss, Pompey. Farewell. Go,
say I sent thee thither. For debt, Pompey? or how?

Elbow. For being a bawd, for being a bawd.

Lucio. Well, then, imprison him. If imprisonment be
the due of a bawd, why, 'tis his right. Bawd is he,
doubtless, and of antiquity too: bawd-born. Farewell, good Pompey. Commend me to the prison, Pompey. You will turn good husband now, Pompey, you
will keep the house.   345

Pompey. I hope, sir, your good Worship will be my
bail.

318 **Caesar** the conqueror of Pompey. 319 **Pygmalion's images** N.
321 **it** F omits. **clutched** i.e. full of money. 322 **tune** temper,
humor. 324 **Trot** contemptuous term for an old woman. 325 **sad**
serious. **trick** fashion. 330–1 **she . . . tub** N. 334 **unshunned**
inevitable. 344 **husband** in its etymological sense, housekeeper.

Lucio. No, indeed will I not, Pompey; it is not the wear. I will pray, Pompey, to increase your bondage: if you take it not patiently, why, your mettle is the more. Adieu, trusty Pompey. 'Bless you, Friar.

Duke. And you.   352

Lucio. Does Bridget paint still, Pompey, ha?

Elbow. Come your ways, sir. Come.

Pompey. You will not bail me then, sir?

Lucio. Then, Pompey, nor now. What news abroad, Friar? What news?

Elbow. Come your ways, sir. Come.

Lucio. Go to kennel, Pompey. Go.

        [Exeunt Elbow, Pompey, and Officers.]

What news, Friar, of the Duke?   360

Duke. I know none. Can you tell me of any?

Lucio. Some say he is with the emperor of Russia; other some, he is in Rome. But where is he, think you?

Duke. I know not where; but wheresoever, I wish him well.   366

Lucio. It was a mad fantastical trick of him to steal from the state, and usurp the beggary he was never born to. Lord Angelo dukes it well in his absence; he puts trangression to't.   370

Duke. He does well in't.

Lucio. A little more lenity to lechery would do no harm in him. Something too crabbed that way, Friar.

Duke. It is too general a vice, and severity must cure it.   375

Lucio. Yes, in good sooth, the vice is of a great kindred; it is well allied. But it is impossible to extirp it quite, Friar, till eating and drinking be put down.

---

349 **wear** fashion. 350 **mettle** spirit, with a quibble. 368 **usurp** wrongfully assume. 377 **extirp** extirpate.

They say this Angelo was not made by man and
woman after this downright way of creation. Is it
true, think you?   381

Duke. How should he be made, then?

Lucio. Some report a sea-maid spawn'd him; some
that he was begot between two stock-fishes. But it is
certain that when he makes water his urine is con-
geal'd ice, that I know to be true. And he is a motion
generative, that's infallible.   387

Duke. You are pleasant, sir, and speak apace.

Lucio. Why, what a ruthless thing is this in him,
for the rebellion of a cod-piece to take away the life
of a man! Would the Duke that is absent have done
this? Ere he would have hang'd a man for the getting
a hundred bastards, he would have paid for the nurs-
ing a thousand. He had some feeling of the sport; he
knew the service, and that instructed him to mercy.

Duke. I never heard the absent Duke much detected
for women; he was not inclin'd that way.   397

Lucio. O, sir, you are deceiv'd.

Duke. 'Tis not possible.

Lucio. Who? Not the Duke? Yes, your beggar of
fifty. And his use was to put a ducat in her clack-
dish. The Duke had crotchets in him. He would be
drunk, too; that let me inform you.

Duke. You do him wrong, surely.   404

Lucio. Sir, I was an inward of his. A shy fellow was
the Duke; and I believe I know the cause of his with-
drawing.

380 **after** according to. 384 **stock-fishes** dried codfish. 386–7
motion generative N. 390 **cod-piece** N. 392 **getting** begetting.
396 **detected** accused. 400–1 **beggar of fifty** beggarwoman fifty
years old. 401–2 **clack-dish** wooden dish with a lid, clacked to
attract attention. 402 **crotchets** odd fancies. 405 **inward** intimate.
shy reserved, fearful.

Duke. What, I prethee, might be the cause?

Lucio. No, pardon. 'Tis a secret must be lock'd within the teeth and the lips. But this I can let you understand, the greater file of the subject held the Duke to be wise.

Duke. Wise! Why, no question but he was.

Lucio. A very superficial, ignorant, unweighing fellow.   415

Duke. Either this is envy in you, folly, or mistaking. The very stream of his life and the business he hath helm'd must, upon a warranted need, give him a better proclamation. Let him be but testimonied in his own bringings-forth, and he shall appear to the envious a scholar, a statesman, and a soldier. Therefore, you speak unskillfully; or, if your knowledge be more, it is much darkened in your malice.

Lucio. Sir, I know him, and I love him.   424

Duke. Love talks with better knowledge, and knowledge with dearer love.

Lucio. Come, sir, I know what I know.

Duke. I can hardly believe that, since you know not what you speak. But, if ever the Duke return— as our prayers are he may—let me desire you to make your answer before him. If it be honest you have spoke, you have courage to maintain it. I am bound to call upon you; and, I pray you, your name?   434

Lucio. Sir, my name is Lucio, well known to the Duke.

409 **must** which must. 411 **greater file** majority. 414 **unweighing** thoughtless. 418 **helm'd** steered. 418 **upon . . . need** were warrant needed. 418–9 **give him a better proclamation** proclaim him to be a better man. 419 **testimonied** attested. 420 **bringings-forth** achievements. 422 **unskillfully** without discernment. 426 **dearer** F *deare*.

Duke. He shall know you better, sir, if I may live to report you.

Lucio. I fear you not.   439

Duke. O! You hope the Duke will return no more, or you imagine me too unhurtful an opposite. But indeed I can do you little harm; you'll forswear this again!

Lucio. I'll be hang'd first. Thou art deceiv'd in me, Friar. But no more of this. Canst thou tell if Claudio die tomorrow or no?   446

Duke. Why should he die, sir?

Lucio. Why? For filling a bottle with a tun-dish. I would the Duke we talk of were return'd again: this ungenitur'd agent will unpeople the province with continency. Sparrows must not build in his house-eaves because they are lecherous. The Duke yet would have dark deeds darkly answered; he would never bring them to light. Would he were return'd! Marry, this Claudio is condemned for untrussing. Farewell, good Friar; I prethee, pray for me. The Duke, I say to thee again, would eat mutton on Fridays. He's not past it yet, and I say to thee, he would mouth with a beggar, though she smelt brown bread and garlic. Say that I said so. Farewell.   460
Exit.

Duke. No might nor greatness in mortality
Can censure 'scape. Back-wounding calumny
The whitest virtue strikes. What king so strong
Can tie the gall up in the slanderous tongue?
But who comes here?   465

---

441 opposite adversary. 448 **tun-dish** funnel. 450 **ungenitur'd** impotent. 455 **untrussing** undoing the trousers. 457 mutton N. 458 **He's . . . thee** N. **not** F *now.* 461 **mortality** human life.

*Enter Escalus, Provost, and [Officers with] Bawd
[Mistress Overdone].*

Escalus. Go, away with her to prison!

Mistress Overdone. Good my lord, be good to me.
Your Honor is accounted a merciful man, good my
lord.   469

Escalus. Double and treble admonition, and still
forfeit in the same kind! This would make mercy
swear, and play the tyrant.

Provost. A bawd of eleven years' continuance, may
it please your Honor.   474

Mistress Overdone. My lord, this is one Lucio's information against me. Mistress Kate Keepdown was
with child by him in the Duke's time; he promis'd her
marriage. His child is a year and a quarter old, come
Philip and Jacob. I have kept it myself, and see how
he goes about to abuse me!   480

Escalus. That fellow is a fellow of much license. Let
him be call'd before us. Away with her to prison! Go
to: no more words. [*Exeunt Officers with Mistress
Overdone.*] Provost, my brother Angelo will not be
alter'd; Claudio must die tomorrow. Let him be furnish'd with divines, and have all charitable preparation. If my brother wrought by my pity, it should
not be so with him.

Provost. So please you, this friar hath been with
him, and advis'd him for th' entertainment of death.

Escalus. Good even, good Father.   491

Duke. Bliss and goodness on you!

Escalus. Of whence are you?

471 forfeit liable to penalty. 479 **Philip and Jacob** N. 487 **wrought
by my pity** acted as mercifully as I would. 490 **entertainment**
expectation.

Duke. Not of this country, though my chance is
 now
To use it for my time. I am a brother
Of gracious order, late come from the See,   495
In special business from his Holiness.

Escalus. What news abroad i' th' world?

Duke. None, but that there is so great a fever on
goodness, that the dissolution of it must cure it.
Novelty is only in request, and it is as dangerous to
be aged in any kind of course, as it is virtuous to be
constant in any undertaking. There is scarce truth
enough alive to make societies secure, but security
enough to make fellowships accurs'd. Much upon this
riddle runs the wisdom of the world. This news is old
enough, yet it is every day's news. I pray you, sir,
of what disposition was the Duke?   507

Escalus. One that, above all other strifes, contended
especially to know himself.

Duke. What pleasure was he given to?

Escalus. Rather rejoicing to see another merry,
than merry at anything which professed to make him
rejoice: a gentleman of all temperance. But leave
we him to his events, with a prayer they may prove
prosperous; and let me desire to know how you find
Claudio prepar'd. I am made to understand that you
have lent him visitation.   517

Duke. He professes to have received no sinister
measure from his judge, but most willingly humbles
himself to the determination of justice; yet had he
framed to himself, by the instruction of his frailty,

494 **time** present time. 495 **See** i.e. of Rome. 499 **dissolution**
death. 500 **only** especially. 503 **security** N. 508 **strifes** endeavors.
514 **to his events** to the outcome of his affairs. 517 **visitation**
priestly visit. 518 **sinister** unjust. 520 **determination** sentence.
521 **framed** fabricated. **instruction** prompting.

many deceiving promises of life, which I, by my good
leisure, have discredited to him, and now is he re-
solv'd to die.   524

Escalus. You have paid the heavens your function,
and the prisoner the very debt of your calling. I
have labor'd for the poor gentleman to the extremest
shore of my modesty; but my brother-justice have I
found so severe, that he hath forc'd me to tell him he
is indeed Justice.   530

Duke. If his own life answer the straitness of his
proceeding, it shall become him well; wherein if he
chance to fail, he hath sentenc'd himself.

Escalus. I am going to visit the prisoner. Fare you
well.   535

Duke. Peace be with you!

           [Exeunt Escalus and Provost.]

He, who the sword of heaven will bear
Should be as holy as severe;
Pattern in himself to know,
Grace to stand, and virtue go;   540
More nor less to others paying
Than by self-offenses weighing.
Shame to him whose cruel striking
Kills for faults of his own liking!
Twice treble shame on Angelo,   545
To weed my vice and let his grow!
O, what may man within him hide,
Though angel on the outward side!
How may likeness made in crimes,
Making practice on the times,   550
To draw with idle spider's strings

525 paid . . . function done your duty toward God. 528 **shore**
limit. **modesty** sense of propriety. 537–58 He . . . contracting N.
540 and virtue go if virtue fail. 549–52 How . . . things N.

Most ponderous and substantial things?
Craft against vice I must apply:
With Angelo tonight shall lie
His old betrothed, but despised: 555
So disguise shall, by th' disguised,
Pay with falsehood, false exacting,
And perform an old contracting.   *Exit.*

Act IV

SCENE 1

Enter Mariana, and Boy singing.

'Take, O take those lips away,
   That so sweetly were forsworn;
And those eyes, the break of day,
   Lights that do mislead the morn:
But my kisses bring again, bring again,
Seals of love, but seal'd in vain, seal'd in vain.'

Enter Duke [disguised as before].

Mariana. Break off thy song, and haste thee quick
    away.
Here comes a man of comfort, whose advice
Hath often still'd my brawling discontent.

                       [Exit Boy.]

I cry you mercy, sir, and well could wish
You had not found me here so musical.   5
Let me excuse me, and believe me so,
My mirth it much displeas'd, but pleas'd my woe.
  Duke. 'Tis good; though music oft hath such a
    charm
To make bad good, and good provoke to harm.   9
I pray you tell me, hath anybody inquir'd for me
here today? Much upon this time have I promis'd
here to meet.

'Take . . . vain' N. 4 cry you mercy beg your pardon. 7 My
mirth . . . woe N. 12 meet be present.

Mariana. You have not been inquir'd after. I have sat here all day. 14

Enter Isabella.

Duke. I do constantly believe you. The time is come even now. I shall crave your forbearance a little; may be I will call upon you anon, for some advantage to yourself.

Mariana. I am always bound to you. *Exit.*

Duke. Very well met, and well come. 20
What is the news from this good deputy?

Isabella. He hath a garden circummur'd with brick,
Whose western side is with a vineyard back'd;
And to that vineyard is a planched gate,
That makes his opening with this bigger key. 25
This other doth command a little door
Which from the vineyard to the garden leads.
There have I made my promise,
Upon the heavy middle of the night,
To call upon him. 30

Duke. But shall you on your knowledge find this way?

Isabella. I have tane a due and wary note upon't.
With whispering and most guilty diligence,
In action all of precept, he did show me
The way twice ore. 35

Duke. Are there no other tokens
Between you 'greed concerning her observance?

Isabella. No, none, but only a repair i' th' dark,
And that I have possess'd him my most stay

15 **constantly** firmly. 22 **circummur'd** walled around. 24 **planched** boarded. 29 **heavy** drowsy. 34 **action all of precept** with instructive gestures. 35 **ore** o'er, over. 36 **observance** i.e. of the instructions Isabella has received. 37 **repair** rendezvous. 38 **possess'd** informed.

Can be but brief; for I have made him know
I have a servant comes with me along,   40
That stays upon me, whose persuasion is
I come about my brother.
  Duke.   'Tis well borne up.
I have not yet made known to Mariana
A word of this. What ho, within! Come forth!

Enter Mariana.

I pray you, be acquainted with this maid.   45
She comes to do you good.
  Isabella.   I do desire the like.
  Duke. Do you persuade yourself that I respect you?
  Mariana. Good Friar, I know you do, and have
    found it.
  Duke. Take then this your companion by the hand,
Who hath a story ready for your ear.   50
I shall attend your leisure, but make haste;
The vaporous night approaches.
  Mariana. Will't please you walk aside?
                Exeunt [*Mariana and Isabella*].
  Duke. O place and greatness! Millions of false eyes
Are stuck upon thee. Volumes of report   55
Run with these false and most contrarious quests
Upon thy doings; thousand escapes of wit
Make thee the father of their idle dream,
And rack thee in their fancies!

Enter Mariana and Isabella.

                Welcome, how agreed?

---

42 **borne up** contrived. 55 **stuck** fixed. **report** rumor. 56 **quests**
inquiries (cries of hounds upon the scent). 57 **escapes** sallies.
59 **rack** distort.

Isabella. She'll take the enterprise upon her, Father,
If you advise it.

Duke.　　　　　It is not my consent,　　　　61
But my entreaty too.

Isabella.　　　　　　Little have you to say
When you depart from him but, soft and low,
'Remember now my brother.'

Mariana.　　　　　　Fear me not.

Duke. Nor, gentle daughter, fear you not at all.　65
He is your husband on a pre-contract.
To bring you thus together, 'tis no sin,
Sith that the justice of your title to him
Doth flourish the deceit. Come, let us go:
Our corn's to reap, for yet our tilth's to sow.　70
　　　　　　　　　　　　　　　　Exeunt.

SCENE 2

Enter Provost and Clown [Pompey].

Provost. Come hither, sirrah. Can you cut off a
man's head?

Pompey. If the man be a bachelor, sir, I can; but
if he be a married man, he's his wife's head, and I
can never cut off a woman's head.　　　　5

Provost. Come, sir, leave me your snatches, and
yield me a direct answer. Tomorrow morning are to
die Claudio and Barnardine. Here is in our prison
a common executioner, who in his office lacks a
helper. If you will take it on you to assist him, it
shall redeem you from your gyves; if not, you shall
have your full time of imprisonment, and your de-

69 flourish gloss over. 70 tilth plowed land N. 6 snatches
quibbles. 9 common public. 11 gyves chains.

liverance with an unpitied whipping, for you have
been a notorious bawd.   14

Pompey. Sir, I have been an unlawful bawd time
out of mind, but yet I will be content to be a lawful
hangman. I would be glad to receive some instruction
from my fellow partner.

Provost. What ho, Abhorson! Where's Abhorson,
there?   20

Enter Abhorson.

Abhorson. Do you call, sir?

Provost. Sirrah, here's a fellow will help you tomorrow in your execution. If you think it meet, compound with him by the year, and let him abide here
with you; if not, use him for the present and dismiss
him. He cannot plead his estimation with you; he
hath been a bawd.

Abhorson. A bawd, sir? Fie upon him! He will dis-
credit our mystery.   29

Provost. Go to, sir: you weigh equally. A feather
will turn the scale.   *Exit.*

Pompey. Pray, sir, by your good favor—for surely,
sir, a good favor you have, but that you have a hanging look—do you call, sir, your occupation a mystery?   35

Abhorson. Ay, sir, a mystery.

Pompey. Painting, sir, I have heard say, is a mystery; and your whores, sir, being members of my
occupation, using painting, do prove my occupation
a mystery. But what mystery there should be in
hanging, if I should be hang'd, I cannot imagine.

13 **unpitied** pitiless. 23 **meet** fitting. **compound** come to terms.
26 **estimation** good reputation. 29 **mystery** craft, trade. 32 **favor**
countenance.

Abhorson. Sir, it is a mystery. 42
Pompey. Proof?
Abhorson. Every true man's apparel fits your thief. If it be too little for your thief, your true man thinks it big enough. If it be too big for your thief, your thief thinks it little enough; so every true man's apparel fits your thief.

Enter Provost.

Provost. Are you agreed? 49
Pompey. Sir, I will serve him, for I do find that your hangman is a more penitent trade than your bawd; he doth oftener ask forgiveness.
Pompey. You, sirrah, provide your block and your ax tomorrow four o'clock. 54
Abhorson. Come on, bawd. I will instruct thee in my trade. Follow.
Pompey. I do desire to learn, sir; and, I hope, if you have occasion to use me for your own turn, you shall find me yare. For, truly, sir, for your kindness I owe you a good turn. 60
Provost. Call hether Barnardine and Claudio.
        Exeunt [Pompey and Abhorson].
Th' one has my pity, not a jot the other,
Being a murtherer, though he were my brother.

Enter Claudio.

Look, here's the warrant, Claudio, for thy death.
'Tis now dead midnight, and by eight tomorrow 65
Thou must be made immortal. Where's Barnardine?
Claudio. As fast lock'd up in sleep as guiltless labor

44-48 Every . . . thief N. 44 true honest. 52 he . . . forgiveness N. 59 yare nimble F *y'are.* 61 hether hither.

When it lies starkly in the traveler's bones.
He will not wake.
 Provost.   Who can do good on him?
Well, go, prepare yourself. [*Knocking within.*] But
  hark, what noise?   70
Heaven give your spirits comfort. [*Exit Claudio.*]
  By and by.
I hope it is some pardon or reprieve
For the most gentle Claudio.

    Enter Duke [*disguised as before*].

           Welcome, Father.
Duke. The best and wholesom'st spirits of the night
Envelop you, good Provost. Who call'd here of late?
Provost. None since the curfew rung.   76
Duke. Not Isabel?
Provost.   No.
Duke. They will, then, ere't be long.
Provost. What comfort is for Claudio?
Duke. There's some in hope.
Provost.   It is a bitter deputy.
Duke. Not so, not so: his life is parallel'd   81
Even with the stroke and line of his great justice.
He doth with holy abstinence subdue
That in himself which he spurs on his power
To qualify in others. Were he meal'd with that   85
Which he corrects, then were he tyrannous,
But this being so, he's just. [*Knocking within.*] Now
  are they come.   [*Exit Provost.*]
This is a gentle provost. Sildom when

68 starkly stiffly. 71 By and by right away (in answer to the
knocking). 82 Even read 'E'en.' stroke and line N. 85 qualify
temper. meal'd stained. 88 Sildom when it is seldom that.

The steeled gaoler is the friend of men. [*Knocking.*]
How now! What noise? That spirit's possess'd with
    haste   90
That wounds th' unsisting postern with these strokes.

[*Enter Provost.*]

Provost. There he must stay until the officer
Arise to let him in; he is call'd up.
  Duke. Have you no countermand for Claudio yet,
But he must die tomorrow?
  Provost.   None, sir, none.   95
  Duke. As near the dawning, Provost, as it is,
You shall hear more ere morning.
  Provost.   Happily
You something know: yet I believe there comes
No countermand. No such example have we.
Besides, upon the very siege of justice,   100
Lord Angelo hath to the public ear
Profess'd the contrary.

Enter a Messenger.

  Duke. This is his Lord's man.
  Provost. And here comes Claudio's pardon.   104
  Messenger. My Lord hath sent you this note, and
by me this further charge: that you swerve not from
the smallest article of it, neither in time, matter, or
other circumstance. Good morrow; for, as I take it,
it is almost day.   109
  Provost. I shall obey him.   [*Exit Messenger.*]
  Duke. [*Aside.*] This is his pardon, purchas'd by
    such sin

89 steeled hardened. 91 **unsisting** unresisting. 97 **Happily** perchance. 100 **siege** seat.

For which the pardoner himself is in:
Hence hath offense his quick celerity,
When it is borne in high authority.
When Vice makes Mercy, Mercy's so extended,   115
That for the fault's love is th' offender friended.
Now, sir, what news?

Provost. I told you. Lord Angelo, belike thinking
me remiss in mine office, awakens me with this un-
wonted putting on—methinks strangely, for he hath
not us'd it before.   121

Duke. Pray you, let's hear.

[*Provost reads*] *The Letter.*

*Whatsoever you may hear to the contrary, let
Claudio be executed by four of the clock; and,
in the afternoon, Barnardine. For my better
satisfaction, let me have Claudio's head sent me
by five. Let this be duly performed, with a
thought that more depends on it than we must
yet deliver. Thus fail not to do your office, as
you will answer it at your peril.*

What say you to this, sir?   132

Duke. What is that Barnardine who is to be executed in th' afternoon?

Provost. A Bohemian born, but here nurs'd up and
bred; one that is a prisoner nine years old.

Duke. How came it that the absent Duke had not
either deliver'd him to his liberty or executed him?
I have heard it was ever his manner to do so.   139

Provost. His friends still wrought reprieves for
him; and, indeed, his fact, till now in the government

120 **putting on** incitement. 136 **prisoner . . . old** prisoner for
nine years. 140 **still** constantly. 141 **fact** crime.

of Lord Angelo, came not to an undoubtful proof.

Duke. It is now apparent?

Provost. Most manifest, and not denied by himself.

Duke. Hath he borne himself penitently in prison?
How seems he to be touch'd?   146

Provost. A man that apprehends death no more
dreadfully but as a drunken sleep: careless, reckless,
and fearless of what's past, present, or to come;
insensible of mortality, and desperately mortal.

Duke. He wants advice.   151

Provost. He will hear none. He hath evermore had
the liberty of the prison: give him leave to escape
hence, he would not. Drunk many times a day, if
not many days entirely drunk. We have very oft
awak'd him, as if to carry him to execution, and
show'd him a seeming warrant for it; it hath not
moved him at all.   158

Duke. More of him anon. There is written in your
brow, Provost, honesty and constancy. If I read it
not truly, my ancient skill beguiles me; but in the
boldness of my cunning I will lay myself in hazard.
Claudio, whom here you have warrant to execute, is
no greater forfeit to the law than Angelo who hath
sentenc'd him. To make you understand this in a
manifested effect, I crave but four days' respite, for
the which you are to do me both a present and a
dangerous courtesy.   168

Provost. Pray, sir, in what?

Duke. In the delaying death.

Provost. Alack! how may I do it, having the hour

142 **undoubtful** certain 148 **dreadfully** with dread. 150 **mortality**
death. **mortal** lacking in any hope of immortality. 151 **advice**
spiritual counsel. 162 **lay . . . hazard** jeopardize myself (a dicing
metaphor). 165–6 **in . . . effect** by presenting concrete evidence.

limited, and an express command, under penalty, to
deliver his head in the view of Angelo? I may make
my case as Claudio's, to cross this in the smallest.

Duke. By the vow of mine order I warrant you, if
my instructions may be your guide. Let this Barnardine be this morning executed, and his head borne to
Angelo.   178

Provost. Angelo hath seen them both, and will discover the favor.

Duke. O! death's a great disguiser, and you may
add to it. Shave the head, and dye the beard; and
say it was the desire of the penitent to be so bar'd
before his death. You know the course is common.
If anything fall to you upon this, more than thanks
and good fortune, by the Saint whom I profess, I
will plead against it with my life.   187

Provost. Pardon me, good Father; it is against
my oath.

Duke. Were you sworn to the Duke or to the
deputy?

Provost. To him, and to his substitutes.

Duke. You will think you have made no offense,
if the Duke avouch the justice of your dealing?

Provost. But what likelihood is in that?   195

Duke. Not a resemblance, but a certainty. Yet
since I see you fearful, that neither my coat, integrity, nor persuasion can with ease attempt you, I
will go further than I meant, to pluck all fears out
of you. Look you, sir; here is the hand and seal of

---

172 **limited** designated. 174 **cross** thwart. 175 **warrant you** guar-
antee your security. 180 **favor** difference in feature. 182 **dye** F
tie N. 183 **bar'd** shaved. 196 **resemblance** probability.

the Duke: you know the character, I doubt not, and
the signet is not strange to you.   202

Provost. I know them both.

Duke. The contents of this is the return of the
Duke. You shall anon over-read it at your pleasure,
where you shall find within these two days, he will
be here. This is a thing that Angelo knows not, for
he this very day receives letters of strange tenor,
perchance of the Duke's death, perchance entering
into some monastery, but by chance nothing of
what is writ. Look, th' unfolding star calls up the
shepherd. Put not yourself into amazement how these
things should be; all difficulties are but easy when
they are known. Call your executioner, and off with
Barnardine's head. I will give him a present shrift
and advise him for a better place. Yet you are
amaz'd, but this shall absolutely resolve you. Come
away; it is almost clear dawn.

                                   Exit [with Provost].

SCENE 3

Enter Clown [Pompey].

Pompey. I am as well acquainted here as I was in
our house of profession: one would think it were
Mistress Overdone's own house, for here be many of
her old customers. First, here's young Master Rash;

201 **character** handwriting. 211 **unfolding star** morning star,
when the flocks leave the fold. 212 **amazement** perplexity. 215
shrift confession and absolution. 217 **resolve** assure. 2 **profession**
business.

78

he's in for a commodity of brown paper and old ginger, nine-score and seventeen pounds, of which he made five marks, ready money. Marry, then ginger was not much in request, for the old women were all dead. Then is there here one Master Caper, at the suit of Master Threepile the mercer, for some four suits of peach-color'd satin, which now peaches him a beggar. Then have we here young Dizzy, and young Master Deepvow, and Master Copperspur, and Master Starve-lackey, the rapier and dagger man, and young Drop-heir that kill'd lusty Pudding, and Master Forthright the tilter, and brave Master Shoe-tie, the great traveler, and wild Half-can that stabb'd Pots, and, I think, forty more; all great doers in our trade, and are now 'for the Lord's sake.'

Enter Abhorson.

Abhorson. Sirrah, bring Barnardine hither.   20

Pompey. Master Barnardine! You must rise and be hang'd, Master Barnardine.

Abhorson. What ho! Barnardine!

Barnardine. [*Within.*] A pox o' your throats! Who makes that noise there? What are you?   25

Pompey. Your friends, sir, the hangman. You must be so good, sir, to rise and be put to death.

Barnardine. [*Within.*] Away! you rogue, away! I am sleepy.   29

Abhorson. Tell him he must awake, and that quickly too.

Pompey. Pray, Master Barnardine, awake till you are executed, and sleep afterwards.

5–9 commodity . . . dead N. 11 peaches impeaches. 16 **tilter** fencer. 17 **Shoe-tie** N. 19 'for . . . sake' cry of prisoners asking alms from jail windows. 25 **what** who.

Abhorson. Go in to him, and fetch him out.   34

Pompey. He is coming, sir, he is coming. I hear his straw rustle.

Enter Barnardine.

Abhorson. Is the ax upon the block, sirrah?

Pompey. Very ready, sir.

Barnardine. How now, Abhorson! What's the news with you?   40

Abhorson. Truly, sir, I would desire you to clap into your prayers: for, look you, the warrant's come.

Barnardine. You rogue, I have been drinking all night; I am not fitted for't.   44

Pompey. O, the better, sir: for he that drinks all night, and is hang'd betimes in the morning, may sleep the sounder all the next day.

Enter Duke [disguised as before].

Abhorson. Look you, sir; here comes your ghostly father. Do we jest now, think you?   49

Duke. Sir, induced by my charity, and hearing how hastily you are to depart, I am come to advise you, comfort you, and pray with you.

Barnardine. Friar, not I: I have been drinking hard all night, and I will have more time to prepare me, or they shall beat out my brains with billets. I will not consent to die this day, that's certain.   56

Duke. O, sir, you must; and therefore, I beseech you look forward on the journey you shall go.

Barnardine. I swear I will not die today for any man's persuasion.   60

Duke. But hear you—

41–2 **clap into** go at once into. 43–4 I . . . **for't** N. 48 **ghostly** spiritual. 55 **billets** blocks of wood.

Barnardine. Not a word: if you have anything to
say to me, come to my ward; for thence will not
I today.   *Exit.*

Enter Provost.

Duke. Unfit to live or die. O gravel heart!   65
After him, fellows: bring him to the block.
              [*Exeunt Abhorson and Pompey.*]
Provost. Now, sir, how do you find the prisoner?
Duke. A creature unprepar'd, unmeet for death,
And to transport him in the mind he is
Were damnable.
Provost.   Here in the prison, Father,   70
There died this morning of a cruel fever
One Ragozine, a most notorious pirate,
A man of Claudio's years—his beard and head
Just of his color. What if we do omit
This reprobate till he were well inclin'd,   75
And satisfy the deputy with the visage
Of Ragozine, more like to Claudio?
Duke. O, 'tis an accident that heaven provides!
Dispatch it presently. The hour draws on
Prefix'd by Angelo. See this be done,   80
And sent according to command, whiles I
Persuade this rude wretch willingly to die.
Provost. This shall be done, good Father, presently.
But Barnardine must die this afternoon.
And how shall we continue Claudio,   85
To save me from the danger that might come
If he were known alive?
Duke.   Let this be done.

63 **ward** cell. 65 **gravel** stony. 69 **transport** i.e. to the next world.
74 **omit** pass by. 79 **presently** immediately. 85 **continue** keep.

Put them in secret holds, both Barnardine and
    Claudio.
Ere twice the sun hath made his journal greeting
To th' under generation, you shall find   90
Your safety manifested.

    Provost. I am your free dependant.

    Duke. Quick, dispatch, and send the head to Angelo.
                               Exit [*Provost*].
Now will I write letters to Angelo—
The Provost, he shall bear them—whose contents 95
Shall witness to him I am near at home,
And that, by great injunctions, I am bound
To enter publicly. Him I'll desire
To meet me at the consecrated fount
A league below the city; and from thence,   100
By cold gradation and well-balanc'd form,
We shall proceed with Angelo.

Enter Provost.

    Provost. Here is the head. I'll carry it myself.

    Duke. Convenient is it. Make a swift return,
For I would commune with you of such things 105
That want no ear but yours.

    Provost.   I'll make all speed. *Exit.*

    Isabella. [*Within.*] Peace, ho, be here!

    Duke. The tongue of Isabel. She's come to know
If yet her brother's pardon be come hither.
But I will keep her ignorant of her good,   110
To make her heavenly comforts of despair,
When it is least expected.

Enter Isabella.

89 **journal** daily. 90 **th' under** the Antipodes; F *yond.* 92 **free
dependant** willing servant. 101 **cold gradation** deliberate degrees.
105 **commune** stressed ´ —.

Isabella.   Ho, by your leave!

Duke. Good morning to you, fair and gracious
daughter.   114

Isabella. The better, given me by so holy a man.
Hath yet the deputy sent my brother's pardon?

Duke. He hath releas'd him, Isabel, from the world.
His head is off and sent to Angelo.

Isabella. Nay, but it is not so.   119

Duke. It is no other. Show your wisdom, daughter,
In your close patience.

Isabella. O! I will to him and pluck out his eyes!

Duke. You shall not be admitted to his sight.

Isabella. Unhappy Claudio! Wretched Isabel!
Injurious world! Most damned Angelo!   125

Duke. This nor hurts him nor profits you a jot.
Forbear it therefore; give your cause to heaven.
Mark what I say, which you shall find
By every syllable a faithful verity.
The Duke comes home tomorrow—nay, dry your
eyes—   130
One of our covent, and his confessor,
Gives me this instance. Already he hath carried
Notice to Escalus and Angelo,
Who do prepare to meet him at the gates,
There to give up their power. If you can, pace your
wisdom   135
In that good path that I would wish it go,
And you shall have your bosom on this wretch,
Grace of the Duke, revenges to your heart,
And general honor.

---

121 **close** secret, i.e. by concealing your suffering. 122 **I will** read
'I'll.' 131 **covent** convent. **confessor** stressed ´ — — ´. 132 **instance** piece of news. 135 **pace** direct. 137 **bosom** heart's desire.

Isabella.   I am directed by you.
Duke. This letter then to Friar Peter give—   140
'Tis that he sent me of the Duke's return.
Say, by this token, I desire his company
At Mariana's house tonight. Her cause and yours,
I'll perfect him withal, and he shall bring you
Before the Duke; and to the head of Angelo   145
Accuse him home and home. For my poor self,
I am combined by a sacred vow
And shall be absent. Wend you with this letter.
Command these fretting waters from your eyes
With a light heart. Trust not my holy order,   150
If I pervert your course. Who's here?

Enter Lucio.

Lucio. Good even. Friar, where's the provost?
Duke. Not within, sir.
Lucio. O pretty Isabella, I am pale at mine heart to
see thine eyes so red: thou must be patient. I am fain
to dine and sup with water and bran. I dare not for
my head fill my belly; one fruitful meal would set
me to't. But they say the Duke will be here tomorrow.
By my troth, Isabel, I lov'd thy brother. If the old
fantastical Duke of dark corners had been at home,
he had lived.   161

[Exit Isabella.]

Duke. Sir, the Duke is marvelous little beholding to
your reports; but the best is, he lives not in them.
Lucio. Friar, thou knowest not the Duke so well

144 **perfect** make him fully acquainted with. 146 **home and home**
sharply, decisively. 147 **combined** bound. 148 **Wend you** go your
way. 156 **fain** compelled. 160 **fantastical** capricious. **of dark corners** i.e. he transacts his affairs in dark corners. 163 **in them**
according to them.

as I do. He's a better woodman than thou tak'st
him for.   166

Duke. Well, you'll answer this one day. Fare ye
well.

Lucio. Nay, tarry, I'll go along with thee. I can
tell thee pretty tales of the Duke.   170

Duke. You have told me too many of him already,
sir, if they be true; if not true, none were enough.

Lucio. I was once before him for getting a wench
with child.

Duke. Did you such a thing?   175

Lucio. Yes, marry, did I; but I was fain to forswear
it. They would else have married me to the rotten
medlar.

Duke. Sir, your company is fairer than honest.
Rest you well.   180

Lucio. By my troth, I'll go with thee to the lane's
end. If bawdy talk offend you, we'll have very little
of it. Nay, Friar, I am a kind of burr: I shall stick.

Exeunt.

SCENE 4

Enter Angelo and Escalus.

Escalus. Every letter he hath writ hath disvouch'd
other.

Angelo. In most uneven and distracted manner. His
actions show much like to madness. Pray heaven

165 **woodman** hunter, i.e. of women. 178 **medlar** a fruit rotten
before it is ripe. 179 **fairer** more amiable. 1 **disvouch'd** contra-
dicted.

MEASURE FOR MEASURE, IV. 4

his wisdom be not tainted. And why meet him at the
gates, and redeliver our authorities there?   6

Escalus. I guess not.

Angelo. And why should we proclaim it in an hour
before his ent'ring, that if any crave redress of injustice, they should exhibit their petitions in the
street?   11

Escalus. He shows his reason for that: to have
a dispatch of complaints, and to deliver us from
devices hereafter, which shall then have no power
to stand against us.   15

Angelo. Well, I beseech you let it be proclaim'd.
Betimes i' th' morn I'll call you at your house. Give
notice to such men of sort and suit as are to meet
him.

Escalus. I shall, sir: fare you well.   20

Angelo. Good night.   *Exit* [*Escalus*].
This deed unshapes me quite, makes me unpregnant
And dull to all proceedings. A deflower'd maid,
And by an eminent body that enforc'd
The law against it! But that her tender shame   25
Will not proclaim against her maiden loss,
How might she tongue me! Yet reason dares her no:
For my authority bears off a credent bulk,
That no particular scandal once can touch   29
But it confounds the breather. He should have liv'd,
Save that his riotous youth, with dangerous sense,
Might in the times to come have tane revenge,

14 devices cunning plots. 16–9 Well . . . night N. 17 Betimes
early. 18 sort and suit rank and standing. 22 unshapes confounds.
unpregnant unapt. 26 her maiden loss loss of her virginity. 27
tongue accuse. dares her no intimidates her into saying nothing.
28 credent bulk weight of credibility. 29 particular personal.
32 tane ta'en, taken.

By so receiving a dishonor'd life
With ransom of such shame. Would yet he had liv'd!
Alack, when once our grace we have forgot,   35
Nothing goes right: we would, and we would not.
                                              Exit.

SCENE 5

Enter Duke [in his own habit] and Friar Peter.

Duke. These letters at fit time deliver me.
The provost knows our purpose and our plot.
The matter being afoot, keep your instruction,
And hold you ever to our special drift,   4
Though sometimes you do blench from this to that,
As cause doth minister. Go call at Flavius' house,
And tell him where I stay; give the like notice
To Valencius, Rowland, and to Crassus,
And bid them bring the trumpets to the gate.   9
But send me Flavius first.
    Friar Peter.   It shall be speeded well. [*Exit.*]

Enter Varrius.

Duke. I thank thee, Varrius; thou hast made good
    haste.
Come, we will walk. There's other of our friends
Will greet us here anon, my gentle Varrius.   *Exeunt.*

34 **he had** read 'he'd.' 1 **me** ethical dative. 4 **drift** purpose. 5
blench turn aside. 9 **trumpets** trumpeters.

SCENE 6

Enter Isabella and Mariana.

Isabella. To speak so indirectly I am loath.
I would say the truth; but to accuse him so,
That is your part. Yet I'm advis'd to do it,
He says, to veil full purpose.
 Mariana.   Be rul'd by him. 4
Isabella. Besides, he tells me that if peradventure
He speak against me on the adverse side,
I should not think it strange, for 'tis a physic
That's bitter to sweet end.
 Mariana. I would Friar Peter—

Enter [Friar] Peter.

Isabella.   O, peace! The friar is come.
Friar Peter. Come, I have found you out a stand
 most fit, 10
Where you may have such vantage on the Duke
He shall not pass you. Twice have the trumpets
 sounded.
The generous and gravest citizens
Have hent the gates, and very near upon
The Duke is ent'ring; therefore hence, away. 15
          Exeunt.

2 **I would** read 'I'd.' 4 **veil full purpose** conceal our full plan.
10 **stand** station. 11 **vantage** advantage of position. 13 **generous**
of noble birth. 14 **hent** reached.

Act V

SCENE 1

*Enter Duke, Varrius, Lords, Angelo, Escalus, Lucio,
[Provost, Officers, and] Citizens at several doors.*

Duke. My very worthy cousin, fairly met.
Our old and faithful friend, we are glad to see you.

Angelo.
}Happy return be to your royal Grace!
Escalus.

Duke. Many and hearty thankings to you both.
We have made inquiry of you; and we hear   5
Such goodness of your justice, that our soul
Cannot but yield you forth to public thanks,
Forerunning more requital.

Angelo.   You make my bonds still greater.

Duke. O, your desert speaks loud, and I should
      wrong it,
To lock it in the wards of covert bosom,   10
When it deserves with characters of brass,
A forted residence 'gainst the tooth of time
And razure of oblivion. Give me your hand,
And let the subject see, to make them know
That outward courtesies would fain proclaim   15
Favors that keep within. Come, Escalus,
You must walk by us on our other hand;
And good supporters are you.

1 **cousin** title of respect. 2 **we are** read 'we're.' 5 **we have** read
'we've.' 10 **wards** prison cells. **covert bosom** i.e. keep it secret in
ιy heart. 11 **characters** letters. 12 **forted** fortified. 13 **razure**
effacement.

89

Enter [Friar] Peter and Isabella.

Friar Peter. Now is your time. Speak loud and
    kneel before him. 19

Isabella. Justice, O royal Duke! Vail your regard
Upon a wrong'd—I would fain have said, a maid!
O worthy Prince, dishonor not your eye
By throwing it on any other object
Till you have heard me in my true complaint
And given me justice, justice, justice, justice! 25

  Duke. Relate your wrongs. In what? By whom? Be
    brief.
Here is Lord Angelo shall give you justice.
Reveal yourself to him.

  Isabella.   O worthy Duke!
You bid me seek redemption of the divel.
Hear me yourself; for that which I must speak 30
Must either punish me, not being believ'd,
Or wring redress from you. Hear me, O hear me,
    here!

  Angelo. My Lord, her wits, I fear me, are not firm.
She hath bin a suitor to me for her brother, 34
Cut off by course of justice—

  Isabella.   By course of justice!

  Angelo. And she will speak most bitterly and
    strange.

  Isabella. Most strange, but yet most truly, will I
    speak.
That Angelo's forsworn, is it not strange?
That Angelo's a murtherer, is't not strange?
That Angelo is an adulterous thief, 40
A hypocrite, a virgin-violator,
Is it not strange, and strange?

20 Vail your regard look down. 34 She hath read 'she'th.'
    90

Duke.   Nay, it is ten times strange.
Isabella. It is not truer he is Angelo
Than this is all as true as it is strange.
Nay, it is ten times true; for truth is truth   45
To th' end of reck'ning.
Duke.   Away with her! Poor soul,
She speaks this in th' infirmity of sense.
Isabella. O Prince, I conjure thee, as thou believ'st
There is another comfort than this world,
That thou neglect me not with that opinion   50
That I am touch'd with madness. Make not impos-
        sible
That which but seems unlike. 'Tis not impossible
But one, the wicked'st caitiff on the ground,
May seem as shy, as grave, as just, as absolute
As Angelo; even so may Angelo,   55
In all his dressings, caracts, titles, forms,
Be an arch-villain. Believe it, royal Prince.
If he be less, he's nothing; but he's more,
Had I more name for badness.
Duke.   By mine honesty,
If she be mad—as I believe no other—   60
Her madness hath the oddest frame of sense,
Such a dependency of thing on thing,
As ere I heard in madness.
Isabella.   O gracious Duke,
Harp not on that; nor do not banish reason
For inequality, but let your reason serve   65
To make the truth appear where it seems hid,
And hide the false seems true.

47 in . . . sense out of a sick mind. 52 unlike improbable.
54 absolute perfect. 56 dressings outward shows. caracts dis-
tinctive marks. 63 ere e'er, ever. 65 inequality injustice. 67 hide
eclipse. seems which seems.

Duke.   Many that are not mad
Have sure more lack of reason. What would you say?

Isabella. I am the sister of one Claudio,
Condemn'd upon the act of fornication   70
To lose his head, condemn'd by Angelo.
I, in probation of a sisterhood,
Was sent to by my brother, one Lucio
As then the messenger—

Lucio.   That's I, and't like your Grace.
I came to her from Claudio, and desir'd her   75
To try her gracious fortune with Lord Angelo
For her poor brother's pardon.

Isabella.   That's he indeed.

Duke. You were not bid to speak.

Lucio.   No, my good lord,
Nor wish'd to hold my peace.

Duke.   I wish you now, then.
Pray you, take note of it, and when you have   80
A business for yourself, pray heaven you then
Be perfect.

Lucio. I warrant your Honor.

Duke. The warrant's for yourself: take heed to't.

Isabella. This gentleman told somewhat of my
               tale—

Lucio. Right.   85

Duke. It may be right, but you are i' the wrong
To speak before your time. Proceed.

Isabella.   I went
To this pernicious caitiff deputy—

Duke. That's somewhat madly spoken.

Isabella.   Pardon it,
The phrase is to the matter.   90

72 probation novitiate. 74 and't like if it please. 79 wish'd
bidden, with a quibble. 90 to applicable to.

Duke. Mended again. The matter: proceed.

Isabella. In brief, to set the needless process by,
How I persuaded, how I pray'd, and kneel'd
How he refell'd me, and how I replied—— 94
For this was of much length—the vild conclusion
I now begin with grief and shame to utter.
He would not, but by gift of my chaste body
To his concupiscible intemperate lust,
Release my brother; and, after much debatement,
My sisterly remorse confutes mine honor, 100
And I did yield to him. But the next morn betimes,
His purpose surfeiting, he sends a warrant
For my poor brother's head.

Duke.   This is most likely!

Isabella. O, that it were as like as it is true!

Duke. By heaven, fond wretch! Thou know'st not
  what thou speak'st, 105
Or else thou art suborn'd against his honor
In hateful practice. First, his integrity
Stands without blemish; next, it imports no reason
That with such vehemency he should pursue
Faults proper to himself. If he had so offended, 110
He would have weigh'd thy brother by himself,
And not have cut him off. Someone hath set you on.
Confess the truth, and say by whose advice
Thou cam'st here to complain.

Isabella.   And is this all?
Then, O you blessed ministers above, 115
Keep me in patience; and with ripen'd time
Unfold the evil which is here wrapt up

92 set . . . by pass over. 94 refell'd refuted. 95 vild vile. 98
concupiscible lewd. 100 remorse pity. 105 fond foolish. 106
suborn'd bribed to bear false witness. 107 practice stratagem.
110 proper belonging.

In countenance! Heaven shield your Grace from woe,
As I, thus wrong'd, hence unbelieved go!

Duke. I know you'd fain be gone. An officer!   120
To prison with her! Shall we thus permit
A blasting and a scandalous breath to fall
On him so near us? This needs must be a practice.
Who knew of your intent and coming hither?

Isabella. One that I would were here, Friar Lodowick.   125

Duke. A ghostly father, belike. Who knows that
Lodowick?

Lucio. My lord, I know him; 'tis a meddling friar.
I do not like the man. Had he been lay, my lord,
For certain words he spake against your Grace
In your retirement, I had swing'd him soundly.   130

Duke. Words against me! This' a good friar,
belike!
And to set on this wretched woman here
Against our substitute! Let this friar be found.

Lucio. But yesternight, my lord, she and that friar,
I saw them at the prison: a saucy friar,   135
A very scurvy fellow.

Friar Peter. Blessed be your royal Grace!
I have stood by, my lord, and I have heard
Your royal ear abus'd. First, hath this woman
Most wrongfully accus'd your substitute,   140
Who is as free from touch or soil with her,
As she from one ungot.

Duke.   We did believe no less.
Know you that Friar Lodowick that she speaks of?

---

118 **countenance** authority. 123 **practice** plot. 128 **lay** a layman.
130 **swing'd** beaten. 131 **This'** this is. 141 **soil** defilement. 142
ungot unborn.

Friar Peter. I know him for a man divine and
   holy—
Not scurvy, nor a temporary meddler,   145
As he's reported by this gentleman;
And, on my trust, a man that never yet
Did, as he vouches, misreport your Grace.
Lucio. My lord, most villainously—believe it.
Friar Peter. Well: he in time may come to clear
   himself,   150
But at this instant he is sick, my lord,
Of a strange fever. Upon his mere request,
Being come to knowledge that there was complaint
Intended 'gainst Lord Angelo, came I hether,
To speak, as from his mouth, what he doth know 155
Is true and false; and what he with his oath
And all probation will make up full clear,
Whensoever he's convented. First, for this woman,
To justify this worthy nobleman,
So vulgarly and personally accus'd,   160
Her shall you hear disproved to her eyes,
Till she herself confess it.
Duke.   Good Friar, let's hear it.

[Isabella withdraws, guarded.] Enter Mariana.

Do you not smile at this, Lord Angelo?
O heaven, the vanity of wretched fools!
Give us some seats. Come, cousin Angelo,   165
In this I'll be impartial. Be you judge
Of your own cause. Is this the witness, Friar?

145 temporary in worldly affairs. 152 **Upon . . . request** solely
because he requested it. 154 **hether** hither. 157 **probation** proof.
158 Whensoever read 'whensoe'er.' **convented** summoned. 160
vulgarly publicly. SD Isabella withdraws N. 166 **be impartial**
take no part.

First, let her show her face, and after speak.

Mariana. Pardon, my lord. I will not show my face
Until my husband bid me.   170

Duke. What, are you married?

Mariana. No, my lord.

Duke. Are you a maid?

Mariana. No, my lord.

Duke. A widow, then?   175

Mariana. Neither, my lord.

Duke. Why, you are nothing, then—neither maid,
widow, nor wife?

Lucio. My lord, she may be a punk; for many of
them are neither maid, widow, nor wife.   180

Duke. Silence that fellow. I would he had some cause
To prattle for himself.

Lucio. Well, my lord.

Mariana. My lord, I do confess I nere was married,
And I confess besides I am no maid: 185
I have known my husband, yet my husband
Knows not that ever he knew me.

Lucio. He was drunk, then, my lord; it can be no
better.   189

Duke. For the benefit of silence, would thou wert so
too!

Lucio. Well, my lord.

Duke. This is no witness for Lord Angelo.

Mariana. Now I come to't, my lord:
She that accuses him of fornication,   195
In selfsame manner doth accuse my husband;
And charges him, my lord, with such a time,
When, I'll depose, I had him in mine arms,
With all th' effect of love.   199

168 her F *your.* 179 **punk** prostitute. 184 **nere** ne'er, never

Angelo. Charges she moe than me?

Mariana.   Not that I know.

Duke. No? You say your husband?

Mariana. Why, just, my lord, and that is Angelo,
Who thinks he knows that he nere knew my body,
But knows he thinks that he knows Isabel's.   204

Angelo. This is a strange abuse. Let's see thy face.

Mariana. My husband bids me. Now I will unmask.

                             [Unveiling.]

This is that face, thou cruel Angelo,
Which once thou swor'st was worth the looking on.
This is the hand which, with a vow'd contract,
Was fast belock'd in thine. This is the body   210
That took away the match from Isabel,
And did supply thee at thy garden-house
In her imagin'd person.

Duke.   Know you this woman?

Lucio. Carnally, she says.

Duke.   Sirrah, no more!

Lucio. Enough, my lord.   215

Angelo. My lord, I must confess I know this woman,
And five years since there was some speech of mar-
       riage
Betwixt myself and her, which was broke off,
Partly for that her promised proportions
Came short of composition, but in chief   220
For that her reputation was disvalued
In levity: since which time of five years
I never spake with her, saw her, nor heard from her,
Upon my faith and honor.

205 abuse deception. 209 **contract** stressed — ´—. 211 **match**
appointment. 212 **supply** gratify. 219 **promised** F *promis'd*. proportions dowry. 220 **composition** agreement. 222 **levity** loose
conduct.

Mariana.   Noble Prince,
As there comes light from heaven and words from
          breath,   225
As there is sense in truth and truth in virtue,
I am affianc'd this man's wife as strongly
As words could make up vows; and, my good lord,
But Tuesday night last gone in's garden-house
He knew me as a wife. As this is true,   230
Let me in safety raise me from my knees
Or else forever be confixed here
A marble monument.

    Angelo.   I did but smile till now:
Now, good my lord, give me the scope of justice—
My patience here is touch'd. I do perceive   235
These poor informal women are no more
But instruments of some more mightier member
That sets them on. Let me have way, my lord,
To find this practice out.

    Duke.   Ay, with my heart;
And punish them to your height of pleasure.   240
Thou foolish Friar, and thou pernicious woman,
Compact with her that's gone, think'st thou thy
          oaths,
Though they would swear down each particular
          saint,
Were testimonies against his worth and credit   244
That's seal'd in approbation? You, Lord Escalus,
Sit with my cousin. Lend him your kind pains
To find out this abuse, whence 'tis deriv'd.
There is another friar that set them on.
Let him be sent for.

232 **confixed** firmly fixed. 234 **scope** free play. 236 **informal**
foolish. 242 **Compact** leagued. 243 **particular** read 'partic'lar.'
244 **against** read 'gainst.'
    98

Friar Peter. Would he were here, my lord; for he
    indeed   250
Hath set the women on to this complaint.
Your provost knows the place where he abides
And he may fetch him.
    Duke.   Go do it instantly. [*Exit Provost.*]
And you, my noble and well-warranted cousin,
Whom it concerns to hear this matter forth,   255
Do with your injuries as seems you best,
In any chastisement. I for a while
Will leave you, but stir not you till you have
Well determin'd upon these slanderers.
    Escalus. My lord, we'll do it throughly.   260
                                      Exit [*Duke*].
Signior Lucio, did not you say you knew that Friar
Lodowick to be a dishonest person?
    Lucio. *Cucullus non facit monachum:* honest in
nothing, but in his clothes; and one that hath spoke
most villainous speeches of the Duke.   265
    Escalus. We shall entreat you to abide here till he
come and enforce them against him. We shall find
this friar a notable fellow.
    Lucio. As any in Vienna, on my word.   269
    Escalus. Call that same Isabel here once again. I
would speak with her. [*Exit an Attendant.*] Pray
you, my lord, give me leave to question; you shall
see how I'll handle her.
    Lucio. Not better than he, by her own report.
    Escalus. Say you?   275
    Lucio. Marry, sir, I think, if you handled her
privately, she would sooner confess: perchance, publicly, she'll be asham'd.

260 **throughly** thoroughly. 263 **Cucullus . . . monachum** the
hood does not make the monk. 268 **notable** worth watching.

*Enter Duke [in his friar's habit], Provost, Isabella
[and Officers].*

Escalus. I will go darkly to work with her.   279

Lucio. That's the way: for women are light at
midnight.

Escalus. Come on, mistress. Here's a gentlewoman
denies all that you have said.

Lucio. My lord, here comes the rascal I spoke of—
here with the provost.   285

Escalus. In very good time. Speak not you to him,
till we call upon you.

Lucio. Mum.

Escalus. Come, sir. Did you set these women on to
slander Lord Angelo? They have confess'd you did.

Duke. 'Tis false.   291

Escalus. How! know you where you are?

Duke. Respect to your great place! And let the
divel

Be sometime honor'd for his burning throne.   294

Where is the Duke? 'Tis he should hear me speak.

Escalus. The Duke's in us, and we will hear you
speak.

Look you speak justly.

Duke. Boldly at least. But O, poor souls,

Come you to seek the lamb here of the fox?

Good night to your redress! Is the Duke gone?   300

Then is your cause gone, too. The Duke's unjust,

Thus to retort your manifest appeal

And put your trial in the villain's mouth

Which here you come to accuse.   304

Lucio. This is the rascal! This is he I spoke of.

279 **darkly** obscurely. 280 **light** wanton, a quibble. 294 **burning
throne** N. 302 **retort** throw back.

Escalus. Why, thou unreverend and unhallow'd
  Friar!
Is't not enough thou hast suborn'd these women
To accuse this worthy man but, in foul mouth,
And in the witness of his proper ear,
To call him villain?   310
And then to glance from him to th' Duke himself,
To tax him with injustice? Take him hence.
To th' rack with him! We'll touse him joint by joint,
But we will know his purpose. What! 'Unjust'!
  Duke. Be not so hot. The Duke   315
Dare no more stretch this finger of mine than he
Dare rack his own: his subject am I not,
Nor here provincial. My business in this state
Made me a looker-on here in Vienna,
Where I have seen corruption boil and bubble   320
Till it orerun the stew. Laws for all faults,
But faults so countenanc'd, that the strong statutes
Stand like the forfeits in a barber's shop,
As much in mock as mark.
  Escalus. Slander to th' state! Away with him to
  prison!   325
  Angelo. What can you vouch against him, Signior
  Lucio?
Is this the man that you did tell us of?
  Lucio. 'Tis he, my lord. Come hither, goodman bald-
pate. Do you know me?   329
  Duke. I remember you, sir, by the sound of your
voice. I met you at the prison in the absence of the
Duke.

309 in . . . ear in his own hearing. 313 touse tear. him F *you*.
318 provincial within his jurisdiction. 321 stew cauldron, brothel.
323–4 forfeits . . . mark N.

101

Lucio. O, did you so? And do you remember what you said of the Duke?

Duke. Most notedly, sir.   335

Lucio. Do you so, sir? And was the Duke a flesh-monger, a fool, and a coward, as you then reported him to be?

Duke. You must, sir, change persons with me, ere you make that my report. You, indeed, spoke so of him; and much more, much worse.   341

Lucio. O thou damnable fellow! Did not I pluck thee by the nose for thy speeches?

Duke. I protest I love the Duke as I love myself.

Angelo. Hark how the villain would close now, after his treasonable abuses!   346

Escalus. Such a fellow is not to be talk'd withal. Away with him to prison! Where is the provost? Away with him to prison! Lay bolts enough upon him, let him speak no more. Away with those giglets too, and with the other confederate companion!   351

[*The Provost lays hands on the Duke.*]

Duke. Stay, sir: stay a while.

Angelo. What! Resists he? Help him, Lucio.

Lucio. Come, sir; come, sir; come, sir. Foh, sir! Why, you bald-pated, lying rascal, you must be hooded, must you? Show your knave's visage, with a pox to you! Show your sheep-biting face, and be hang'd an hour! Will't not off?   358

[*Pulls off the friar's hood, and discovers the Duke.*]

Duke. Thou art the first knave that ere mad'st a Duke.

First, Provost, let me bail these gentle three.   360

335 **notedly** particularly. 345 **close** come to terms. 347 **withal** with. 350 **giglets** lewd women. 357 **sheep-biting** skulking.

[*To Lucio.*] Sneak not away, sir, for the friar **and**
    you
Must have a word anon. Lay hold on him.
  Lucio. This may prove worse than hanging.
  Duke. [*To Escalus.*] What you have spoke I par-
    don. Sit you down,
We'll borrow place of him. [*To Angelo.*] Sir, by
    your leave.   365
Hast thou or word, or wit, or impudence
That yet can do thee office? If thou hast,
Rely upon it till my tale be heard,
And hold no longer out.
  Angelo.   O my dread lord!
I should be guiltier than my guiltiness   370
To think I can be undiscernible,
When I perceive your Grace, like power divine,
Hath look'd upon my passes. Then, good Prince,
No longer session hold upon my shame,
But let my trial be mine own confession.   375
Immediate sentence, then, and sequent death
Is all the grace I beg.
  Duke.   Come hither, Mariana.
Say, wast thou ere contracted to this woman?
  Angelo. I was, my lord.   379
  Duke. Go take her hence, and marry her instantly.
Do you the office, Friar—which consummate,
Return him here again. Go with him, Provost.

            Exit [*Angelo, with Mariana, Friar Peter,
                      and Provost*].

  Escalus. My lord, I am more amaz'd at his dishonor
Than at the strangeness of it.

366 or . . . or either . . . or. 369 **hold . . . out** maintain no
longer silence. 371 **be undiscernible** remain unrevealed. 373
passes devices. 374 **session hold** sit in judgment. 381 **consummate**
performed.

Duke.   Come hither, Isabel.
Your friar is now your prince. As I was then   386
Advertising and holy to your business,
Not changing heart with habit, I am still
Attorney'd at your service.

Isabella.   O, give me pardon,
That I, your vassal, have employ'd and pain'd   389
Your unknown sovereignty.

Duke.   You are pardon'd, Isabel.
And now, dear maid, be you as free to us.
Your brother's death, I know, sits at your heart,
And you may marvel why I obscur'd myself,
Laboring to save his life, and would not rather
Make rash remonstrance of my hidden power   395
Than let him so be lost. O most kind maid,
It was the swift celerity of his death
That brain'd my purpose: but peace be with him.
That life is better life, past fearing death,   399
Than that which lives to fear. Make it your comfort,
So happy is your brother.

Enter Angelo, Mariana, [Friar] Peter, Provost.

Isabella.   I do, my lord.
Duke. For this new-married man approaching here,
Whose salt imagination yet hath wrong'd
Your well-defended honor, you must pardon
For Mariana's sake. But as he adjudg'd your
        brother—   405
Being criminal, in double violation

386 **Advertising** (stressed — $\acute{-}$ — $\grave{-}$) and **holy** ministering and
devoted. 388 **Attorney'd** i.e. as an advocate or special pleader.
391 **free** generous. 393 **marvel** probably to be read 'mar'l.'
395 **rash remonstrance** hasty manifestation. 397 **celerity** read
'celer'ty.' 398 **brain'd** shattered. 401 **So** thus. 403 **salt** lascivious.
406 **criminal** guilty.

Of sacred chastity, and of promise-breach,
Thereon dependent, for your brother's life—
The very mercy of the law cries out
Most audible, even from his proper tongue, 410
'An Angelo for Claudio, death for death!'
Haste still pays haste, and leisure answers leisure,
Like doth quit like, and Measure still for Measure.
Then, Angelo, thy fault's thus manifested,
Which though thou wouldst deny, denies thee van-
    tage. 415
We do condemn thee to the very block
Where Claudio stoop'd to death, and with like haste.
Away with him!
   Mariana.   O, my most gracious lord!
I hope you will not mock me with a husband.
   Duke. It is your husband mock'd you with a hus-
    band. 420
Consenting to the safeguard of your honor,
I thought your marriage fit. Else imputation,
For that he knew you, might reproach your life
And choke your good to come. For his possessions,
Although by confutation they are ours, 425
We do instate and widow you with all,
To buy you a better husband.
   Mariana.   O my dear lord!
I crave no other, nor no better man.
   Duke. Never crave him; we are definitive.
   Mariana. Gentle my liege—
   Duke.   You do but lose your
    labor. 430

---

413 Measure . . . Measure N. 415 vantage the advantage of
any such denial. 422 imputation censure. 425 confutation the fact
of Angelo's proven guilt N. 426 instate and widow give you as a
widow's legacy. 429 definitive firmly resolved.

Away with him to death! [*To Lucio.*] Now, sir, to
  you.

  Mariana. O my good lord! Sweet Isabel, take my
      part:
Lend me your knees, and, all my life to come,
I'll lend you all my life to do you service.   434

  Duke. Against all sense you do importune her:
Should she kneel down in mercy of this fact,
Her brother's ghost his paved bed would break,
And take her hence in horror.

  Mariana.   Isabel,
Sweet Isabel, do yet but kneel by me:
Hold up your hands, say nothing, I'll speak all.   440
They say best men are moulded out of faults,
And, for the most, become much more the better
For being a little bad: so may my husband.
O, Isabel! will you not lend a knee?

  Duke. He dies for Claudio's death.

  Isabella. [*Kneeling.*]   Most bounteous
      sir,   445
Look, if it please you, on this man condemn'd,
As if my brother liv'd. I partly think
A due sincerity governed his deeds,
Till he did look on me. Since it is so,
Let him not die. My brother had but justice,   450
In that he did the thing for which he died:
For Angelo,
His act did not oretake his bad intent,
And must be buried but as an intent   454
That perish'd by the way. Thoughts are no subjects,

436 fact evil deed. 437 **paved bed** i.e. vaulted with stone N.
442 **for the most** in most cases. 448 sincerity read 'sincer'ty.'
455 **Thoughts are no subjects** thoughts are not punishable by
the state.

Intents but merely thoughts.

Mariana.   Merely, my lord.

Duke. Your suit's unprofitable: stand up, I say.
I have bethought me of another fault.
Provost, how came it Claudio was beheaded
At an unusual hour?

Provost.   It was commanded so.   460

Duke. Had you a special warrant for the deed?

Provost. No, my good lord; it was by private message.

Duke. For which I do discharge you of your office.
Give up your keys.

Provost.   Pardon me, noble lord:
I thought it was a fault, but knew it not,   465
Yet did repent me, after more advice;
For testimony whereof, one in the prison,
That should by private order else have died
I have reserv'd alive.

Duke.   What's he?

Provost.   His name is Barnardine.

Duke. I would thou hadst done so by Claudio.   470
Go, fetch him hither: let me look upon him.

                [Exit Provost.]

Escalus. I am sorry, one so learned and so wise
As you, Lord Angelo, have still appear'd,
Should slip so grossly, both in the heat of blood,
And lack of temper'd judgment afterward.   475

Angelo. I am sorry that such sorrow I procure;
And so deep sticks it in my penitent heart
That I crave death more willingly than mercy.
'Tis my deserving, and I do entreat it.

466 advice consideration. 473 still always.

107

Enter Barnardine and Provost, Claudio [muffled],
Julietta.

Duke. Which is that Barnardine?
Provost.   This, my lord.
Duke. There was a friar told me of this man.   481
Sirrah, thou art said to have a stubborn soul,
That apprehends no further than this world,
And squar'st thy life according. Thou'rt condemn'd:
But, for those earthly faults, I quit them all,   485
And pray thee take this mercy to provide
For better times to come. Friar, advise him:
I leave him to your hand. What muffled fellow's that?
Provost. This is another prisoner that I sav'd,
Who should have died when Claudio lost his head—
As like almost to Claudio as himself.   491
                              [*Unmuffles Claudio.*]
Duke. [*To Isabella.*] If he be like your brother, for
   his sake
Is he pardon'd, and, for your lovely sake—
Give me your hand and say you will be mine—
He is my brother too. But fitter time for that.   495
By this Lord Angelo perceives he's safe—
Methinks I see a quick'ning in his eye.
Well, Angelo, your evil quits you well.
Look that you love your wife; her worth, worth
   yours.
I find an apt remission in myself,   500
And yet here's one in place I cannot pardon.

482 **thou art** read 'thou'rt.' 484 **squar'st** shapes. 485 **quit** remit.
487 **advise** give spiritual counsel. 498 **quits** requites. 500 **apt**
remission ready forgiveness. 501 **in place** present.

[*To Lucio.*] You, sirrah, that knew me for a fool, a
    coward,
One all of luxury, an ass, a madman:
Wherein have I so deserv'd of you,
That you extol me thus? 505
   Lucio. 'Faith, my lord, I spoke it but according to
the trick. If you will hang me for it, you may; but I
had rather it would please you, I might be whipped.
   Duke. Whipp'd first, sir, and hang'd after.
Proclaim it, Provost, round about the city, 510
If any woman wrong'd by this lewd fellow—
As I have heard him swear himself there's one
Whom he begot with child—let her appear,
And he shall marry her. The nuptial finish'd,
Let him be whipp'd and hang'd. 515
   Lucio. I beseech your Highness, do not marry me
to a whore. Your Highness said even now, I made
you a Duke. Good my lord, do not recompense me in
making me a cuckold. 519
   Duke. Upon mine honor, thou shalt marry her.
Thy slanders I forgive; and therewithal
Remit thy other forfeits. Take him to prison,
And see our pleasure herein executed.
   Lucio. Marrying a punk, my lord, is pressing to
death, whipping, and hanging. 525
   Duke. Slandering a prince deserves it.
               [*Exeunt officers with Lucio.*]
She, Claudio, that you wrong'd, look you restore.
Joy to you, Mariana! Love her, Angelo.
I have confess'd her and I know her virtue. 529

---

503 luxury lechery. 506–7 according to the trick as a joke. 522
Remit . . . forfeits cancel your other punishments. 524–5 pressing to death i.e. by the placing of heavy weights on the chest.

Thanks, good friend Escalus, for thy much goodness:
There's more behind that is more gratulate.
Thanks, Provost, for thy care and secrecy;
We shall employ thee in a worthier place.
Forgive him, Angelo, that brought you home
The head of Ragozine for Claudio's: 535
Th' offense pardons itself. Dear Isabel,
I have a motion much imports your good,
Whereto if you'll a willing ear incline,
What's mine is yours, and what is yours is mine.
So, bring us to our palace, where we'll show   540
What's yet behind, that's meet you all should know.
                                        [*Exeunt.*]

531 behind to come. gratulate pleasing. 537 motion proposal.

NOTES

Act I, Scene 1

[The Actors' Names] Based upon the list of characters appended to the Folio text of the play. Bracketed names appear in the text but not on the list. The list supplies the Duke's name, Vincentio, which does not appear in the text.

Act I The Folio divides this play into acts and scenes throughout. These divisions are 'theatrical'—that is, they are adapted to the special conditions of the Elizabethan stage. Modern editors generally do not begin a new scene at I.2.118, and generally divide Act III into two scenes.

8-9 But . . . work Possibly two half-lines have been omitted here, but the text is not unintelligible as it stands. The Duke has just praised Escalus for a knowledge of government exceeding his own. Nothing remains, then, except that Escalus apply his best abilities to his *sufficiency*—that is, his fitness for government—and let them work together.

30-1 as to . . . thee 'As to justify you in wasting your energy upon the mere cultivation of your virtues or in limiting the effect of your virtues to your own character' (Durham).

32-3 Heaven . . . themselves Cf. Matthew 5:15, 'Neither do men light a candle, and put it under a bushel, but on a candlestick; and it giveth light unto all that are in the house.'

36-40 Nature . . . use 'She requires and allots to herself the same advantages that creditors usually enjoy—thanks for the endowments she has bestowed, and extraordinary exertions in those whom she has thus favored, by way of interest (use)' (Malone).

41 one . . . advertise One who can, in his own right, make known his abilities as my deputy.

42 Hold Possibly reflecting stage business. The Duke extends the commission to Angelo, whose initial reluctance to accept it

is emphasized by Shakespeare. Some editors, however, believe that the Duke is here exhorting Angelo to hold fast to those virtues he has just described him as possessing. There is little to choose between the two interpretations. It is quite likely that the text has been cut.

53–5 Our . . . value The need for our hasty departure is so compelling that we must give it preference over important matters which would otherwise require our attention.

Act I, Scene 2

16 petition . . . peace The authorized form of grace under Queen Elizabeth ended with the words, 'God save our Queen and Realm, and send us peace in Christ.'

22 proportion There are many contemporary references to the tediously long graces fashionable at the time. Lucio is quibbling on one of the meanings of the word 'meter.'

32 three-pil'd Three-piled—that is, deep-napped—velvet was velvet of the very finest quality. The First Gentleman quibbles on this meaning of the term and *pil'd* meaning 'peeled' or 'bald,' with reference to one of the supposed effects of the French Disease, syphilis.

36–9 and . . . thee Lucio mockingly interprets the First Gentleman's *feelingly* (l. 35) as 'painfully,' and so as a confession of a mouth-sore stemming from venereal infection. He therefore says that, although he will start a round of healths in his name, he will avoid drinking after him: that is, out of the same cup.

46–7 I . . . to In the Folio, this speech as well as the preceding one is given to Lucio. Pope was the first of a succession of editors to give the speech to the First Gentleman, from whom it seems slightly more appropriate in view of the subsequent dialogue. In this case, the First Gentleman's remark (ll. 53–4) must be interpreted as whimsy. Lucio capitalizes on another verbal indiscretion.

89 woman The verb 'to do' (see the preceding line) was frequently used in this bawdy sense by Elizabethans. Cf. the name Mistress Overdone.

91 Groping . . . river *Peculiar* means 'privately-owned' and fishing in private waters constituted poaching. One way of catch-

112

ing trout was to tickle them out of their hiding-places. *Peculiar* had also acquired a colloquial meaning of 'mistress.'

94 maid 'Maids' are the young of skate and other fish and, as Wilson points out, Pompey had just mentioned 'groping for trouts.' The explanation, if correct, adds little point and much coarseness to the quibble.

98 suburbs That is, outside the walls of the city, the customary location for Renaissance brothels. The *suburbs* of London were notorious for them.

115–6 Thomas Tapster Mistress Overdone addresses Pompey by the name commonly given, in Shakespeare's day, to any tapster.

SD Enter Provost . . . Gentlemen The Folio begins a new scene at this point, perhaps an evidence of revision for, if ll. 86–118 were not present in an earlier text of the play, the Folio division could be defended. The transition from ll. 1–85 to 119 ff. would then have been sharp enough to warrant a new scene.

125 words of heaven The *words of heaven*, according to Henley, are those found in Romans 9:15, 'For he [God] saith to Moses, I will have mercy on whom I will have mercy, and I will have compassion on whom I will have compassion.' In addition, the passage reflects the conventional Renaissance belief that the ruling prince was a viceroy of God. The meaning, then, would seem to be: the demigod—in this case, Angelo—can make us pay exactly (*by weight*) for our offenses, and his judgments, by virtue of his deputed authority, are as uncontrollable as those of Heaven itself.

137 mortality The Folio reading. Most editors emend to *morality*. But the word *morality* does not appear elsewhere in Shakespeare whereas *mortality* appears often. The word is ultimately derived from Latin *mortalitas* which Cooper (*Thesaurus*, 1578) defines: 'Mortality, frailety, estate subject to decay.'

150 she . . . wife In Shakespeare's day, there were two types of betrothal contract: a contract in words of the future tense (*sponsalia per verba de futuro*) and a contract in words of the present tense (*sponsalia per verba de praesenti*). The former was roughly equivalent to the modern 'engagement' and could be broken off at will. The latter constituted valid and binding matrimony in the eyes of the law. Consummation of the marriage, however, was not to take place before the union had received the benediction of the church, or its licensed representative. 'The husband and wife who have intercourse with each other before the church has blessed their marriage, sin and should be put to penance; they will be compelled by spiritual censures to celebrate their marriage before the face of the church; but they were married already when they exchanged a consent *per verba de praesenti* . . .' (Pollock and Maitland, *The History of English Law*, 1911, 2,372–3). Claudio's contract was clearly *de praesenti*. Technically, therefore, Claudio was guilty of fornication, but it must be added that Shakespeare's contemporaries would have regarded his sin as highly venial. Despite the teaching of the church, cohabitation on the basis of unblessed *de praesenti* contracts was widely practiced.

161 fault . . . newness The meaning of this highly compressed phrase cannot be communicated in a few words. 'Whether it be the fault of newness, a fault arising from the mind being dazzled by a new authority, of which the new governor had yet had only a glimpse . . .' (Malone).

187 prone and speechless dialect The phrase is usually interpreted as an instance of hendiadys—silently earnest or eager. It is difficult, however, to find a precise meaning for *prone*, perhaps because Shakespeare deliberately makes it ambiguous: *prone*, suggesting the posture of supplication, a familiar meaning of Latin *pronus*, but with overtones of an indelicate sexual connotation it seems to have had for Elizabethans. The play is full of such double-entendres.

Act I, Scene 3

20 steeds The Folio has *weedes*, which badly confuses the metaphor, although the reading can be defended. Most editors have adopted the emendation in the text, first suggested by Theobald. Cf. the preceding scene, ll. 162–5.

21 slip The Folio reading, which most editors emend to *sleep*. But the Elizabethan pronunciation of the two words was virtually identical and, in fact, *sleep* was sometimes spelled *slip*. See Helge Kökeritz, *Shakespeare's Pronunciation* (1953), pp. 146,

191. Both meanings are in this passage metaphorically appropriate—perhaps reflecting Shakespeare's intention.

37-9 for . . . punishment For we virtually bid people abuse their liberties when evil deeds are permitted to pass without punishment.

42-3 And . . . slander The Folio reads *fight* for *sight* and *do in slander* for *do it slander*. The emended reading was first proposed by Hanmer. The meaning seems to be that, while Angelo is accomplishing the necessary reforms in the name of the Duke, the latter's nature will remain so completely out of sight that no slander can possibly attach itself to his name.

Act I, Scene 4

32 lapwing A bird notorious for its trickery in leading hunters away from its young. Lucio makes a distinction between what he says and what he really feels,—'tongue far from heart.'

49 marry Sexual intercourse on the basis of an unblessed *de praesenti* contract could be partly expiated by a subsequent celebration of the marriage 'in the face of the church.'

72-6 Doth . . . have These lines have been rearranged by modern editors. In the Folio, the lines end with *so*, *already*, *warrant*, *poor*, *good*. The words *for his* (l. 74) are contracted into *For's* in the Folio.

Act II, Scene 1

22-3 what . . . thieves Angelo has just said that justice can penalize only those offenses which are known to it. But there is no way for justice (*the laws*) to know when thieves pass judgment on thieves.

39 brakes of vice The Folio reading *brakes of ice* has never been convincingly defended. The emendation adopted in the text was first proposed by Rowe. However enigmatic the phrasing may be, the general meaning is clear from the context: 'Some escape from a thicket-like tangle of vices without punishment; others are condemned for a single fault.'

89-90 stew'd prunes There seems to have been a theory that this fruit was effective both in the prevention and cure of venereal

115

disease, hence its popularity in brothels. Perhaps word-play is involved, too. 'Stews' was a common Elizabethan term for 'brothel.'

130 Bunch of Grapes It was the custom in Elizabethan times to give such names to the different rooms of an inn.

175–6 Justice or Iniquity? That is, Elbow or Pompey. There is a glancing allusion here to the old morality plays, in some of which the Vice is actually named Iniquity.

209 draw you A quibble on the name Froth as well as on 'hang, draw, and quarter.' They will *draw you*—that is, empty you, deprive you of all your money and possessions.

222 bum The buttocks, but also the fantastically stuffed trunk hose which emphasized the buttocks and which were very much in vogue at the time.

249 bay A unit of measurement in contemporary architecture. 'Applied to a house,' the NED says, 'it appears to be the space lying under one gable, or included between two party walls.' The bays of the Globe Theater were twelve and a half feet square. See John C. Adams, *The Globe Playhouse*, pp. 20–1.

255–6 I shall . . . you The reference is to the decisive defeat of Pompey by Caesar at the battle of Pharsalus in 48 B.C.

273 put . . . upon't It was the practice for the ward or parish to choose its own constable; the latter, if he wished, might then pay someone else to act as his deputy.

Act II, Scene 2

40–1 To fine . . . actor *To fine* means 'to punish.' Angelo asserts that justice would be nothing if, instead of punishing the criminals, its sole function was to condemn their crimes—crimes already condemned in the statute books.

142–3 She . . . it Here the two meanings of *sense*, upon which Shakespeare plays over and over again, are found in close juxtaposition. The lines recall I.2.186–90.

160 prayers cross As Isabella has just used the term *Honor*, it is a title of respect. Taking the word in its normal sense, Angelo pretends to see in Isabella's remark a prayer at cross purposes with the wish which has formed in his own heart. There

is probably also an oblique reference to the Lord's Prayer—
'Lead us not into temptation, but deliver us from evil.'

169 **Corrupt . . . season** I am corrupted by those very qualities which make her virtuous, just as it is the same sun which
makes carrion putrid and the violet lovely and fragrant.

173 **evils** It has been said that privies were once known as
evils but the NED does not record this meaning. To support the
general conception, there is a scriptural parallel in 2 Kings 10:27.

Act II, Scene 3

40–2 **O . . . horror** Some editors would read *law* for *love*. But
the meaning seems clear enough. Their illicit love has injured
both Claudio and Julietta in that it has brought Claudio a sentence of death and respited Julietta a comfortless life, almost
worse than death itself. In Shakespeare's source-play, Whetstone's *Promos and Cassandra*, Polina, the counterpart of Julietta,
in a long soliloquy, blames love for her misfortunes and those of
her condemned lover (Part I, Act V, Scene 3).

Act II, Scene 4

16–17 **Let's write . . . crest** For *Is't not* (Warburton, Hanmer)
the Folio reads '*Tis not*. The horn is the devil's crest. In *As You
Like It* (IV.2.14–15), Jacques sings of a horn which is also a crest.
Playing on his own name (*good Angel*), Angelo here seems to be
drawing a parallel between himself and the devil, the master-
hypocrite, perhaps in his self-revulsion identifying himself with
the devil, as Iago with other feelings does in *Othello*.

32 **know** In his mind, Angelo translates Isabella's innocent
'I have come to know your pleasure' into the language of sexual
gratification. To *know* a woman was to have sexual relations
with her.

46–9 **'tis . . . one** That is, it is no worse wrongfully to take
away the life of a man who has been legitimately born than it is
to beget an illegitimate child. The coining metaphor is further
developed. For 'meanes' as a variant spelling of 'mints,' see
Kökeritz, *Shakespeare's Pronunciation*, p. 215.

50 **'Tis . . . earth** 'What you have stated is undoubtedly the

117

divine law: murder and fornication are both forbid by the canons of scripture; but on earth the latter offence is considered as less heinous than the former' (Malone).

58 for **accompt** That is, we are not called to such strict account for the sins which are forced upon us as for those we commit voluntarily. Only the number of *compell'd sins*, therefore, has real significance.

80 **enshield** Dover Wilson would read *enshelled*, calling attention to Ben Jonson's *Masque of Blackness* (produced Jan. 5, 1605), in which the female masquers, one of whom was Queen Anne, made their appearance in a large concave shell resembling mother-of-pearl.

122–3 **If . . . weakness** Angelo has just admitted that all men are frail, and *thy weakness* is the weakness of the male sex: 'If no one else has shared my brother's weakness, if he alone has inherited the male frailty to which you refer, then let him die.'

127–8 **Men . . . them** The primary meaning, as Wilson saw, is suggested by the preceding metaphor. Women are as fragile as mirrors and, like mirrors, they too *make forms*—that is, men. Hence, when men take advantage of woman's frailty, they are marring the sex which brought them into being.

145–7 **I . . . others** 'Your virtue assumes an air of licentiousness, which is not natural to you, on purpose to try me' (Steevens). This speech explains why Isabella at first receives Angelo's blunt declaration of love (l. 141) so calmly.

Act III, Scene 1

9 **skyey influences** The received opinion in Shakespeare's day was that the stars and planets influenced not only weather conditions but the affairs and lives of men. A man's fate was in his 'stars.' Cf. the note to III.1.24–5.

14–15 **For . . . baseness** 'For all the conveniences and comforts you possess are provided by the base offices and occupations of others.' But the phrase 'Are nurs'd by baseness' may mean 'Are cherished out of low and selfish motives.'

16–17 **For . . . worm** Editors generally take *worm* in its common Elizabethan sense of 'snake.' But by the *poor worm*, Shakespeare may mean the grave or coffin worm to which, by analogy with 'snake,' he ascribes a forked tongue in a delicate mockery of man's pretensions to valor.

24–5 **For . . . moon** 'Your temperament is influenced in many strange directions by the operation of the moon.' The moon, a symbol of mutability, was believed to affect human character and conduct.

32–4 **Thou . . . both** 'When we are young, we busy ourselves in forming schemes for succeeding time, and miss the gratifications that are before us; when we are old, we amuse the languor of age with the recollection of youthful pleasures or performances: so that our life, of which no part is filled with the business of the present time, resembles our dreams after dinner, when the events of the morning are mingled with the designs of the evening' (Johnson).

34–6 **for . . . Eld** A passage which has never been satisfactorily explained, possibly because it may be corrupt. Perhaps 'in your youth you are forced into a dependence on old age, and are like palsied eld in begging alms.' The central idea is that, in our youth, when we are in a position to enjoy life, we lack the means to do so. By the time we are old and rich, we have lost the power of enjoyment.

SD Enter Isabella Folio stage entrances tend to reflect playhouse conditions. It takes a few moments for the actor, entering from back or side, to reach the center of the stage. Modern editors often find it convenient to drop Folio entrances a few lines.

53 **SD** Modern editors indicate that the Duke and Provost leave the stage at this point but the Folio gives no 'Exeunt.' Nor does the Folio provide a re-entry for the Duke at l. 151. Probably the Duke and Provost simply withdraw to one side of the stage or, if the action of the scene was initiated on the inner stage, to the outer stage.

69–70 **Though . . . scope** Though you were free to range over the wide world, you would still be mentally confined to the idea of your own ignominy.

94 **prenzie** The only two occurrences of this word in the language, according to the NED, appear here within the space of a

few lines. Cf. *prenzie guards* in l. 97. There has been no satisfactory elucidation of the word's meaning. The context seems to require a meaning akin to 'puritanical' or 'prim.' Hotson, however, believes that *prenzie* is Shakespeare's translation of the now obsolete Italian word for 'prince' (*prenze*) and that *prenzie guards* means therefore 'prince-robes, clothes with rich trimming.' The explanation is not very convincing.

123 region The conception of Hell as alternating between severe cold and intense heat was medieval in origin. Both Dante (*Inferno*, canto VI) and Milton (*Paradise Lost*, II, 587–603) draw upon the conception.

216–7 between . . . solemnity The contract of Angelo, like that of Claudio, was of the *de praesenti* type, constituting legal matrimony. Also, like that of Claudio, it had not been solemnized 'in the face of the church.'

272 SD *Exit* Modern editors, with the exception of Wilson, begin a new scene at this point, although one is not designated in the Folio and, in fact, is scarcely necessary. Isabella makes her exit, but the Duke remains on stage and is present when Elbow and his officers enter with their prisoner, Pompey.

278–9 two usuries Procuring and moneylending. Contemporary references show that moneylenders were accustomed to wear gowns furred in this manner. Here the fox skin connotes craft and the lamb skin, innocence.

286 brother father The Duke good-humoredly mocks Elbow's awkward form of address. Elbow was probably represented on the stage as old and doddering.

313 His . . . waist Elbow makes capital of the fact that the hempen rope which Franciscan friars wore as a girdle was also the kind of rope generally used in hangings.

319 Pygmalion's images According to legend, Pygmalion made a statue of a woman so beautiful that he fell in love with it. When he embraced it, the statue came to life. Lucio mocks the tendency of bawds to exaggerate the beauty and chastity of the prostitutes they represent. 'Have you no women to sell who are as beautiful and unstained as Pygmalion's statue when it first came to life?'

330–1 she . . . tub Pompey quibbles on two kinds of tubs: one for corning beef, the other, into which salt was put, for sweating individuals suffering from venereal disease. Hence, *powder'd* (l. 333) means 'salted.'

386–7 **motion generative** A puppet was known as a *motion*. Lucio seems to imply that, although Angelo has the organs of generation, he makes no more use of them than if he were a puppet.

390 **cod-piece** A baggy and often indelicately conspicuous appendage to the front of the breeches.

457 **mutton** The primary reference is to fasting on Fridays during Lent, but Lucio glances at another meaning of *mutton* common at the time, 'prostitute.'

458 **He's . . . thee** Hanmer's emendation. The Folio reads 'He's now past it, yet (and I say to thee),' which can be defended. But the context suggests that the emended reading is preferable. Lucio, furthermore, is not one to qualify his remarks. For Shakespeare to have him do so here would be out of character.

479 **Philip and Jacob** The feast of St. Philip and St. James was celebrated on May 1. Jacobus is the Latin equivalent of James.

503 **security** The Duke alludes to the practice of one friend standing security for another, which often led to broken friendships when bonds were forfeited.

537–58 **He . . . contracting** Many critics believe these octosyllabic couplets were not written by Shakespeare. There is some clumsiness in the phrasing and in general no clear purpose would seem to be served by a chorus at this point. Wilson, while believing that the verse itself is un-Shakespearean, calls attention to the similarity between this chorus and the Gower choruses in *Pericles*. The problem appears insoluble.

549–52 **How . . . things** A most difficult passage and perhaps corrupt. Editors attempt to construe it with the preceding verses, but it might be better to view the lines as interrogatory and transitional. This interpretation is supported by the Folio punctuation of the passage, restored in the present edition. The Duke asks himself how, by adopting spider-like methods of deceit, roughly similar to those of Angelo ('Craft against vice' and 'Pay with falsehood, false exacting'), he can take advantage of the current situation to encompass (*To draw* meaning 'draw together') the *substantial* ends he had earlier outlined to Isabella (see III.1.252–6). Angelo has made the relationship between Claudio and Julietta a criminal one and it is by a 'likeness made in crimes'—that is, by the device of the bed-trick—that the Duke hopes to ensnare Angelo.

Act IV, Scene 1

Take . . . vain This song appears also in Fletcher's *Bloody Brother* (V.2) with, however, the addition of a second stanza. There is no way of knowing whether Shakespeare or Fletcher was its author. The most likely explanation is that Shakespeare wrote the song as we have it in this play and that then Fletcher added the new (and more erotic) stanza to make the song conform to his special purposes in *The Bloody Brother*. On this point, see William R. Bowden, *The English Dramatic Lyric, 1603–42*, p. 28.

7 My mirth . . . woe That is, the music did not make me mirthful but served only to assuage my sorrow.

70 tilth Folio *tithe's*, for which no editor has been able to find a satisfactory meaning. The emendation, first proposed by Warburton, restores both sense and point to the proverb-like saying.

Act IV, Scene 2

44–8 Every . . . thief The Folio ends Abhorson's speech with *thief* (l. 44) and gives the rest of it to Pompey. The alteration, first made by Capell, has been adopted by almost all subsequent editors. The argument of the hangman is based upon the fact that it was customary for Elizabethan hangmen to inherit the clothing worn by their victims at the time of execution. His reasoning, as Heath pointed out, runs exactly parallel to that of Pompey. 'As the latter puts in his claim to the whores, as members of his occupation, and, in virtue of their painting, would enroll his own fraternity in the mystery of painters; so the former equally lays claims to the thieves, as members of his profession, and in their right, endeavors to rank his brethren, the hangmen, under the mystery of fitters of apparel, or tailors.'

52 he . . . forgiveness Another custom of hangmen was to ask forgiveness from those they were about to execute.

82 stroke and line Angelo's manner of life is consistent with

122

his ideals of rendering justice; he practices what he preaches. There may be a quibble on *stroke* (blow of the executioner's ax) and *line* (the hangman's cord).

182 **dye** The Folio reading *tie* can be defended, but see Act IV, Scene 3, ll. 73–4. Harrison suggests that to tie a beard was to trim it short. The emendation adopted in the text was first proposed by Simpson.

Act IV, Scene 3

5–9 **commodity . . . dead** By Act of Parliament in 1571, not more than 10 per cent interest could be charged on loans. Moneylenders, however, could, and frequently did, evade the statute by the legal device known as 'commodities.' Before making a loan of cash, the moneylender would require the borrower to purchase a 'commodity' of goods, usually of little or no value. Thus, in the case of Master Rash, the 'commodity' was 'brown paper and old ginger.' For this he paid £197 and received a loan of five marks (£3.6s.8d.). But, unfortunately, there turned out to be no market for the ginger, since all the old women, who were notoriously fond of it, had died. Pompey, as usual, is indulging his penchant for lighthearted exaggeration.

17 **Shoe-tie** The significance of this name is explained by a passage in Nashe's *Unfortunate Traveller* (McKerrow, 2, 300–1), quoted by Hart and Wilson. 'From Spaine what bringeth our Traveller? . . . I have not yet tucht all, for he hath in either shoo as much taffatie for his tyings as wold serve for an ancient; which serveth him (if you wil have the mysterie of it) of the owne accord for a shoo-rag.'

43–4 **I . . . for't** To take the life of a man when he had not confessed, and been absolved from, his sins was to place his eternal life in jeopardy. So Hamlet will not kill King Claudius while he is praying but prefers to wait until he is 'drunk asleep or in his rage' or in the performance of some act 'That hath no relish of salvation in't.'

Act IV, Scene 4

16–9 **Well . . . night** Set as prose in the Folio, possibly a printer's mistake. The passage is easily translated into blank

123

verse and in many editions it is so rearranged. In this case, the end words for the successive lines would be *proclaim'd, house, suit, well*.

Act V, Scene 1

SD **Isabella withdraws** The Folio has no stage direction to indicate that Isabella leaves the stage at this time. Yet the Duke, at l. 242, refers to her as *gone* and, at l. 270, Escalus orders that Isabella be called *here once again*. She is given a re-entry at l. 278. Capell was the first to establish her exit at l. 162 and modern editors have followed his precedent. Despite the remarks of Friar Peter, l. 161, that the Duke will hear Isabella 'disproved to her eyes,' the latter seems not to have heard the testimony of Mariana. See ll. 282–3. The problem appears insoluble on the basis of available evidence. Wilson suggests that there may have been some tampering with the text at this point.

294 **burning throne** The Duke implies that the devil has ascended the seat of justice in the person of Angelo—'another version,' comments Hart, 'of the good angel on the devil's crest.'

323–4 **forfeits . . . mark** The *forfeits*, as Hart shows, 'were teeth extracted by barbers who doubled as dentists. To advertise their dual function, barbers were wont to hang teeth on a string and exhibit them in their shops. Thus, the extracted teeth stand in the same relation to the 'strong statutes' as the 'threat'ning twigs of birch' in I.3.24.

413 **Measure . . . Measure** Cf. Matthew 7:2. 'For with what judgment ye judge, ye shall be judged: and with what measure ye mete, it shall be measured to you again.' And see the next three verses in Matthew.

425 **confutation.** So Folio. Most editors emend to 'confiscation.' In the longhand of the time, the letters 'c' and 't' looked very much alike and it is easy to see how the compositor could have made a mistake, reading 'confutation' for 'confiscation.' The Folio reading, however, can be defended.

437 **paved bed** Common graves were not *paved*. Hart believes there may be a reference to the 'custom' of burying executed criminals under the stone flooring of the jail. But it seems more likely that the Duke is alluding to the family crypt or vault.

APPENDIX A

Text and Date

It is now generally accepted that there was a performance of *Measure for Measure* at Court on St. Stephen's Day, Dec. 26, 1604. Probably the play as we know it was finished earlier in the same year. Two apparent references to King James (I.1.67–72; II.4.26–30) and a possible reference to the plague year of 1603 (I.2.84) suggest that at least portions of the play were written after March 14, 1603, when James ascended the English throne. But the alleged references are by no means certain, and recently J. Dover Wilson has complicated the problem of a date for *Measure for Measure* by arguing that the play shows evidence of one or more revisions over a period of years. On the whole, however, the style would seem to support the belief that Shakespeare gave the play its final shaping in 1604.

There is no evidence that *Measure for Measure* was published during Shakespeare's lifetime. Consequently, the Folio of 1623 provides the only authoritative text. Unfortunately, the condition of this text entirely justifies Wilson's conclusion that the copy from which it was printed was not an autograph or playhouse manuscript but the work of a rather careless transcriber, who may even have assembled the play from the 'parts' of individual actors. Many entrances and exits are omitted from the Folio text and the stage directions are very thin—facts which give some plausibility to the 'assemblage' theory.

The present edition is based, therefore, upon the text of the First Folio. Emendations have been sparingly introduced. A few obvious printer's errors and mislineations are silently corrected. Otherwise, all departures from the Folio text are duly recorded. Significant emendations are discussed in the notes.

APPENDIX B

Source

Measure for Measure remains one of Shakespeare's most puzzling plays. Revaluations of the play in the last twenty years have greatly enriched our understanding of its thought and poetry, but each new interpretation seems to have raised almost as many questions as it has answered. It is therefore especially gratifying to know the direct source of *Measure for Measure*. Such a source will always furnish interesting materials for a study of Shakespeare's methods and may often suggest fruitful approaches to the problem of interpretation.

The direct source of *Measure for Measure* is George Whetstone's *The right excellent and famous Historye of Promos and Cassandra: Divided into Commical Discourses*, in two parts, published in 1578. The play was apparently never acted. Four years later, Whetstone published a prose version in a collection of short stories called *An Heptameron of Civill Discourses*. Whetstone himself had derived his plot from one of the tales in the *Hecatommithi* of Giraldi Cinthio, published in Sicily in 1565. At some time before 1573, the latter had also dramatized the tale in a play entitled *Epitia*. It is possible that Shakespeare knew the Cinthio versions, and it is all but certain that he knew the *Heptameron*, narrated by 'Madame Isabella,' which may have suggested the name of his heroine. But the only essential debt is to the play of *Promos and Cassandra*.

Whetstone makes the city Julio, in Hungary, the setting for his drama. It begins with the reading of letters from Corvinus, King of Hungary, designating one Promos as the new deputy-governor of Julio and giving him full powers 'to weede from good the yll.' In his speech of acceptance, Promos stresses the

126

need for judicial integrity and impartiality. 'Each shall be doomde,' he says, 'even as his merite is,' but he pointedly asserts the desirability of tempering justice with mercy. Then, as in *Measure for Measure*, the reader is transported into the heart of the city for a glance at the prevailing lawlessness. Sexual corruption is especially evident. We are introduced to Lamia, a notorious strumpet and her 'man,' Rosko, the prototypes of Mistress Overdone and Pompey. From Rosko we learn that Promos has already acted; he has revived an old law making fornication a capital offense and a young man named Andrugio has been arrested and sentenced to death. Lamia is distressed by this piece of news, envisaging a hopeless life of chastity and poverty, but Rosko heartens her with the information that Phallax, the deputy's 'secondary,' is notoriously susceptible to 'lace mutton.' In the meantime, Andrugio appeals to his sister, Cassandra, to intercede on his behalf before the governor. She quickly consents. In the first of two interviews with Promos, she pleads with him to 'over-rule the force of lawe with mercie' and urges as extenuating factors her brother's 'yong yeares,' his over-mastering passion, and his intention to marry his mistress, Polina. Promos tells her to return on the morrow. Cassandra, it immediately develops, has moved him more by her person than by her eloquence. In a brief soliloquy following her departure, he laments the 'sodaine change' her beauty and 'modest wordes' have wrought in him. Promos now reveals his passion for Cassandra to Phallax, and is advised by the latter to offer Cassandra a choice of alternatives: either she must yield up her body to the governor or her brother must die. Confronted with this choice on the occasion of their second meeting, Cassandra indignantly tells Promos 'my selfe wyll dye ere I my honor stayne.' The governor's promise of a subsequent marriage is spurned, and Cassandra hurries off to inform her brother of the new development. Unlike Claudio in *Measure for Measure*, Andrugio shows no trace of horror at the vile offer of the governor. Arguing that 'in forst faultes is no intent of yll,' he begs Cassandra to do as Promos wishes.

Up to this point in the action, the events of *Promos and Cassandra* are closely paralleled by those in *Measure for Measure*.

But now Shakespeare and Whetstone part company. Cassandra at length yields to her brother's entreaties and makes the sacrifice which she has been led to believe will save his life. But she is mistaken. Promos fulfills neither of his two promises; he makes it clear that he has no intention of marrying her and, instead of releasing her brother, gives order that he be executed forthwith and his head presented to Cassandra on a platter. A friendly jailer, however, frees Andrugio, who betakes himself to the woods. For the head of Andrugio, he substitutes 'A dead man's head that suffered th' other day,' and it is this head which he displays to Cassandra. Distraught with grief, Cassandra now resolves to go to King Corvinus with the whole story. This resolution is made at the end of Act IV, Scene 4, of the First Part. Not until the last scene of the Second Part is final justice meted out.

Between these limits, the action moves sluggishly. The alliance between corruption in government, represented by Phallax, and corruption in civil life, represented by Lamia and Rosko, has produced a flourishing immorality. As Shakespeare was later to do, Whetstone intersperses his main action with subplot scenes designed to illustrate this immorality. Corvinus arrives in the city at the end of Act I (of the Second Part) and, shortly afterwards, issues a proclamation announcing his intention to sit in judgment upon grievances. First, Phallax is exposed; Corvinus orders his goods confiscated and strips him of his office. Then Cassandra comes forward and lodges her accusation against the governor. For having unjustly done Andrugio to death, Promos receives the sentence of execution; but he must first marry Cassandra 'to repayre hir honour.' Cassandra now undergoes an astonishing change of heart.

> Nature wyld mee my brother love; now dutie commaunds mee
> To preferre before kyn or friend, my husband's safetie.

Meanwhile Andrugio has heard of the death sentence passed upon Promos, and magnanimously resolves to give himself up in order that he may not see Cassandra 'plunged in distres.' Promos is already on his way to execution when Andrugio, in a timely arrival, reveals his true identity to the king. Impressed by this unselfish action, Corvinus sets Andrugio free after extracting a promise that he will marry Polina. A repentant Promos fares even better. At Cassandra's request, the king not only restores him to his freedom but—surprisingly—to his office as well. And on this pleasant note the play ends.

The plot of Promos and Cassandra has much to recommend it, and no reader will fail to notice the extent to which Shakespeare is indebted to it. But it has one grave flaw. The marriage of Cassandra to her seducer and the would-be murderer of her brother is as distasteful as it is psychologically unsound. Whetstone's attempt to motivate it by representing Cassandra as falling in love with Promos succeeds only in drawing attention to its initial absurdity. It was clearly his recognition of this flaw which led Shakespeare to make his most striking alteration in the plot of the original story. By introducing the Mariana story and the device of the bed-trick, he contrives to save the virtue of his heroine Isabella and, at the same time, does no disservice to Mariana, whose love for Angelo, it is made clear, had triumphantly survived the passage of time and his original dislike for her. Shakespeare's only other major alteration is the increased scope he gives to the activities of the Duke. In the old play, 'Corvinus, King of Hungary' is simply the agent by means of which the action is finally resolved—a *deus ex machina*. In *Measure for Measure*, the powerful figure of the Duke in the background, in touch at all times with the developing situation and always controlling it, transfers our main attention from the plot to the issues which have set it in motion.

The theme of Whetstone's play is weakly defined and executed. Indeed, if the reader is not alert, he tends to lose sight of the theme altogether until suddenly confronted with it in the parting advice which King Corvinus gives Promos.

Henceforth, forethinke of thy forepassed faultes,
And measure grace with Justice evermore.
Unto the poore have evermore an eye,
And let not might out countenaunce their right.
Thy officers trust not in every tale,
In cheife, when they are meanes in strifes and sutes:

129

> Though thou be just, yet coyne maye them corrupt;
> And if by them thou dost injustice showe,
> Tys thou shalt beare the burden of their faultes.

As these lines suggest, for Whetstone the idea that the good governor should temper strict justice with mercy is ancillary to the more general propositions that 'might' should not be confused with 'right' and that the ruler is ultimately responsible for the actions of his subordinates. It was the mercy theme, however, which commended itself to Shakespeare's poetic imagination, and around which he carefully constructed his play. To this theme Shakespeare attached a dignity and importance for which there is no precedent in Whetstone. It may be added that *Measure for Measure* is the only play of Shakespeare with a thematic title.

APPENDIX C

Reading List

R. W. CHAMBERS, 'The Jacobean Shakespeare and *Measure for Measure*,' Annual Shakespeare Lecture of the British Academy, London, 1937.

FRANCIS FERGUSSON, 'Philosophy and Theatre in *Measure for Measure*,' *Kenyon Review*, *14* (1952), 102–20.

G. WILSON KNIGHT, *The Wheel of Fire*, London, 1930.

HELGE KÖKERITZ, *Shakespeare's Pronunciation*, New Haven, 1953.

MARY LASCELLES, *Shakespeare's 'Measure for Measure*,' London, 1953.

WILLIAM W. LAWRENCE, *Shakespeare's Problem Comedies*, New York, 1931.

F. R. LEAVIS, 'The Greatness of *Measure for Measure*,' *Scrutiny*, *10* (1941–2), 234–47.

CLIFFORD LEECH, 'The "Meaning" of *Measure for Measure*,' *Shakespeare Survey*, *3* (1951), 66–73.

ELIZABETH M. POPE, 'The Renaissance Background of *Measure for Measure*,' *Shakespeare Survey*, *2* (1950), 62-82.

SIR ARTHUR QUILLER-COUCH, Introduction, pp. vii–xliii, to the New Cambridge ed. of *Measure for Measure*, Cambridge, 1922.

E. M. W. TILLYARD, *Shakespeare's Problem Plays*, London, 1950.

D. A. TRAVERSI, '*Measure for Measure*,' *Scrutiny*, *11* (1942–3), 40–58.